A systematic approach to Vedic Mathematics

• Sutras • Upasutras • Vidhis • Arithmetic.

Priti Gorsia Chawla

First Published in April 2022

ISBN: 978-93-5611-186-8

BLUEROSE PUBLISHERS

www.bluerosepublishers.com

info@bluerosepublishers.com

+91 8882 898 898

Cover Design:

Muskan

Typographic Design:

Sachvesh Srivastava

Distributed by: BlueRose, Amazon, Flipkart

Table of Contents

FOREWORD

For as long as I can remember, in my academic years and beyond, I have maintained a keen interest in Mathematics. If there was a problem that a friend, niece/nephew or sibling could not solve, I was over eager to try and would not rest until I found the solution. In all these years, I was unaware of Vedic Mathematics as a subject. I had purchased books on the same, but they were an enigma to me. I would learn some concept from the book, practice a few sums, move to the next concept and promptly forget the previous learned concept. I often wondered why that was. If they were easy shortcut tricks to solve mathematical problems, why were they so forgettable?

One day, while on YouTube, I came across a talk by Dr. S. K.Kapur, who was explaining the concept of Vedic Mathematics, and how it was important for a student to learn more about it. When he proposed his theory on Vedic Geometry as a study of 6 spaces as compared to the 3 spaces study of line, square and cube taught in schools and colleges today, I realised that our scriptures carried a lot of records of very advanced mathematics, science, engineering and architecture. To an extent that when the Brahmins carried out 'Yagnas' in the ancient times, the 'Hawankund' construction was different for different purposes of the yagna. The construction of the same were perfectly explained in the Atharva Veda, the fourth and last Veda based on application-based information.

The 6-spaces study formed the basis of the science of the Galaxy, the Planets and the various components of our world and also were the root of astronomy, astrology, Ayurveda, architecture etc.. The 6-spaces also represent the 6 chakras of our body and the scriptures on these form the base of medicine and yes – surgery too. Did you, for instance know that General Surgery, Plastic Surgery and Rhinoplasty are well elucidated in the scriptures that are over 6000 years old?

The 3 dimensions that we study today, form the 'Triloki Vidya' of line, square and cube and represent the earth, air and water while the other 3 spaces, that we are not aware of, form the 'Tridevi Vidya' representing Hypercubes 4, 5 & 6 referring to Brahma, Vishnu & Shiva. The study of the Tridevi Vidya requires a lot of research and understanding of the scriptures and is beyond the scope of our current education system.

It, also, made me realise that the constant invasions in our country, over the past 300 years, have robbed the student, today, of the knowledge of these very scriptures as the powers that were, at that time, did not understand them and hence, were not included in the curriculum. There were, however, a few scholars who adamantly studied them and tried to explain them to the best of their abilities. Even then, I feel a lot has been lost in translation and I wish we were taught and equipped with the language skills to understand them. Whatever was difficult for the invaders of that time, was ignored and over a period of time, we lost touch with our very own roots.

Vedic Mathematics, as we know it today, was the result of years of research and practice by Swami Thirthaji, a Shankaracharya from Puri.

His incomplete works informed us of sixteen mathematical formulae known as the' **Ganita Sutras**' and thirteen corollaries of the said formulae known as the '**Upasutras**'. They were in sentence forms, and the formulae were in the Devnagari script, where each alphabet represented a number. These formulae cover the entire scope of modern mathematics and beyond. The regular practice of these, makes it possible for the student to solve simple, as well as, complex problems very quickly and accurately. The calculations involved are simple to understand and to remember, if one has an understanding of the formulae and their corollaries.

Vedic mathematics is not 'magic' as each 'shortcut' has a perfect explanation. What we learn today of Vedic Maths is the very basics of the system and hence, has to be very simple so as to speed up more complicated calculations. The system taught today, when incorporated with modern mathematics, is said to be an excellent brain development program as:

a) The student can solve problems quickly and accurately
b) It helps to develop the student's interest, concentration, focus, visualisation, reasoning, logic and decision making skills

Apart from the above, the student also develops a keen interest in the subject as calculations are uncomplicated and easy.

The principles introduced in this system apply to all branches of mathematics including arithmetic, algebra, geometry, trigonometry and calculus. Instead of performing long, drawn out calculations, the student can solve problems in a matter of seconds and in one or two steps. Difficult operations, such as, multiplication of large numbers, converting fractions into decimals, squaring, finding square roots and cube roots, division of long numbers, writing down multiplication tables of large numbers and also finding the day of a month of any given year over 2000 years can be done in a single line or two.

Another advantage of this system is that it encourages the student to calculate from left to right, most of the time, instead of the traditional right to left method of Modern Mathematics. We read and write from left to right and even call out numbers from left to right as a result of which, the student feels comfortable while using this system.

Yet another book on Vedic Mathematics? One might ask this question and it would be a valid one. I have read most of them and the one thing that puzzled me was that they were slightly difficult to follow. So, this is an effort to hopefully allow the student or the reader to understand the concepts simply put and in a more systematic manner. I have attempted to explain the same, to the best of my abilities, in this book. It is divided into two parts. The first part deals with the Sutras and Upasutras with translations, explanations and their applications, as also, some special methods or 'vidhis' used in the calculation process. The second part includes 17 chapters of Vedic arithmetic, including all mathematical operations, checking devices and time and calendar calculations. I have included some worked out examples with a few practice exercises of all the concepts explained. It is my humble request, that the student or trainer attempt to create a lot more exercises for practice on their own for the concepts to become clear. I hope this proves useful for the student, as well as, the teacher.

Priti Chawla

PART I

SUTRAS

&

UPASUTRAS

TRANSLATION

EXPLANATION

APPLICATION

SPECIAL VIDHIS

SUDHA

VINCULUM

BEEJANK

DHVAJANK

DVANDVA YOG

SUTRAS & UPASUTRAS

The Vedic Mathematical system is said to have been derived from the 'Atharva Veda'. The first three Vedas viz. Rig Veda, Yajur Veda and Sama Veda are said to be scriptures containing 'pure' knowledge and the fourth, Atharva Veda is 'application-based' knowledge and is the basis of all applications of science and technology.

Each Veda is assigned an 'Upaveda' and the fourth Veda's Upaveda is 'Sthapatya' meaning 'sthapana' or 'to establish'. This Upaveda contains the knowledge of all sciences, mathematics, engineering architecture, astrology, astronomy, ayurveda and so on.

The appendix or 'parisishta' of the Atharva veda is said to contain 16 mathematical formulae and 13 corollaries. '**Sutra**' or 'string' is the name given to the mathematical formula and '**Upasutra**' denotes the corollary in Vedic Mathematics. A sutra is unique in that it is not a numerical formula but is stated in words, for e.g. ' ***All from nine last from ten***'-is one such formula.

To get a deeper understanding of the Sutras, one must have knowledge of the Devnagri Alphabet system where all alphabets are assigned a number. Since all the formulae are given in words in the Devnagri script, the alphabets held in these are important. This translation is again beyond the scope of this book. So we will work with the fact that there are sixteen sutras and 13 upasutras in this system. A translation of the sutra/ upasutra, its general explanation and application are given herein.

A. SUTRAS

Sutra 1 : "Ekadhikena Purvena"

Translation: '*By one more than the previous*'

Application & Explanation:

The first sutra is said to be the source of all following sutras. The first word of the sutra 'Ekadhikena' is composed of 9 alphabets and written from 1 to 9. The 1 is derived from one more than 'shunya' or 0. The total number of alphabets in the sutra is 16 representing the 16 sutras. The sum total of number of factors in the numbers from 1 to 16 is 29 and represents the 16 sutras and 13 upasutras. This sutra is the basis for development of the number system as we know it and holds the principles of all mathematical operations.

For the convenience of students of modern mathematics, we will restrict to this sutra being used in:

a) Finding the squares of numbers ending with 5

For e.g. $(25)^2 = (2*3) \mid 5^2 = 6 \mid 25 = 625$

Here the sign '|' is not an operation sign, rather it is used to split the number 25 into 2 | 5. The left hand digit or tens place digit is then multiplied by one more than itself i.e. 2*(2+1) = 6 and the right hand digit is squared i.e. $5^2 = 25$. The answer is then 625.

b) Finding the product of two numbers whose sum of digits in the units place is 10 and all other digits are same.

For e.g. $28*22 = 2*3 \mid 8*2 = 6 \mid 16 = 616$

Here, the units digits add up to 10 and the tens digits are the same, hence we take the tens place digit and multiply it with its next number (one more than the previous) i.e. 2*(2+1) = 6 and multiply the numbers in the units place i.e. 8*2=16. Therefore, the answer is 616.

c) **Converting vulgar fractions, whose denominator ends with 9, to decimals.** This can be done in two ways: Division and Multiplication.

i. By Division:

e.g. Convert 1/19 to decimal.

Here the denominator ends with 9. To simplify the division method, we find a modified divisor. In this case, the digit before 9 is 1, we take 2 the number after one (**Ekadhika**) as per the Sutra and this will be the modified divisor. This divisor will be used to solve the fraction.

So, $1/19=0.1/2=0.{}_{1}0{}_{0}5{}_{1}2{}_{0}6{}_{0}3{}_{1}1{}_{1}5{}_{1}7{}_{1}8{}_{0}9{}_{1}4{}_{0}7{}_{1}3{}_{1}6{}_{0}8{}_{0}4{}_{0}2{}_{0}1{}_{1}0\ldots$

The divisor is taken as 2, the dividend is 0.1 as 2 is in tens position, the quotient is 0.0 and the remainder is 1. The small numbers given in subscript depict the remainder of every division operation by 2 and is placed before the quotient. The division method is continued till the cycle of numbers is repeated.

Therefore,1/19=0.052631578947368421/0526315….. numbers are repeated.

<u>ii. By Multiplication</u>:

Taking the same example above, the modified multiplier is 2. This operation is carried out from right to left. Place the dividend number to the right most position and multiply by 2 moving to the left.

Hence, $1/19=0.{}^{1}05{}^{1}263{}^{1}1{}^{1}5{}^{1}7{}^{1}89{}^{1}47{}^{1}3{}^{1}68421$

The superscript numbers denote the excess to be carried over.

Note: If the denominator of the fraction does not end in 9 but in 1,3 or 7, they can be converted by multiplying both the numerator and denominator by 9, 3 or 7 respectively, to fulfil the requirement. For e.g. 1/23 can be converted by multiplying, both the numerator and denominator by 3 to get 3/69 and the modified divisor/multiplier will be 6+1=7.

Sutra- 2: "Nikhilam Navatahscharamam Dasatah"

Translation: '*All from nine and last from ten*'

Application & Explanation:

To understand this concept, one needs to understand base numbers and complement numbers. Base numbers are 10 and powers of 10 such as 10^2, 10^3…10^n. All multiples of base numbers like 20, 30…..90, 200, 300…900 etc. are known as sub-bases. Complement numbers are two numbers that add up to a base or sub-base number. Complement numbers of base 10 are 9+1, 8+2, 7+3, 6+4 and 5+5 as they all add up to 10.

This Sutra is used for:

a) **Subtracting numbers from base/ sub-base numbers** :

For e.g.(i) 1000 – 675 = 325.

Here the base is 10^3=1000. To subtract 675 from the base we simply reduce the number to the left of the first 0 by 1 and deduct each digit, from the left, by 9 and the last digit from 10. The answer 325, also gives us the complement of 675 for base 1000.

(ii) 5000 – 748 = 4252.

5000, a multiple of base 1000(1000*5=5000), is a sub base number. To subtract 748 from this number, we reduce 5000 to 4000 and then from left to right, deduct each digit 7 & 4 from 9 and the last digit 8 from 10, to get 4252.

b) **Multiplying numbers close to a base number**:

Numbers close to a base could be lower or higher than the base. Like 997 is lower than and 1012 is higher than the base 1000. To find how much higher or lower the number is to the base, deduct the number from the base to find its **deviation (d)**. So, d of 997 = 997-1000 = -3 and 1012 =1012-1000 = +12. This deviation is important to understand, to multiply large number close to the base quickly.

For e.g. To multiply 998*997, we write the numbers down on the left hand side, with their deviations on the right hand side. On the left hand side (LHS), solve crosswise by adding the number with the deviation of the other number. On the right hand side (RHS), multiply the deviations. The resulting product here, has to be written down as the same number of digits as there are 0s in the base.

Here the base = 1000, d of 998 is -2 and of 997 is -3

LHS= 998 | -2 = RHS

997 | -3

(998-3) or (997-2) | -2 * -3 = 995 | (00)6.

Since base =1000 there will be 3 digit places on the right. So, **998*997 = 995006**

Sutra -3: " Urdhva Tiryagbhyam"

Translation: '*Vertically and Crosswise*"

Application & Explanation:

This third sutra is mainly used in **multiplying any two numbers**.

For e.g To multiply 2digit number* 2 digit number – The total number of digits in this problem is 4. Therefore, the number of steps to complete the multiplication operation will be 4 -1 =3.

- The first step is to 'vertically' multiply the units place numbers and place the end digit of product in the units place in the solution and carry over the rest of the product to the tens place

- The second step is to 'crosswise' multiply the tens place digit of the first number with the units place digit of the second number and add this to the product of units place digit of first number and tens place digit of second number. Add the carried over number from the product of the first step. Place the end digit of this solution in the tens place and carry over the rest.

- The third and final step, is to 'vertically' multiply the digits in the tens place, add the carried over number and place before the tens place in the solution.

For 28*64

Step 1 - 8*4 = 32 or $_{3}2$ where 2 is the units digit and 3 is carried over. (Vertically)

Step 2 - 2*4 + 8*6 + 3(carried over) = 8 + 48 + 3= 59 written as $_{5}92$ (Criss- cross wise)

Step 3 – 2*6 + 5(carried over) = 12 + 5 = 17 (Vertically).

Therefore, **28*64= 1792**.

This is the basic concept and can be used to multiply large numbers in one or two lines simply and quickly. This will be explained in more details in the multiplication chapter of this book.

Sutra 4 : " Paravartya Yojayet"

Translation : ' *Transpose and apply*'

Application & Explanation:

The division of numbers where the divisor is just under a base and has large numbers uses the 'Nikhilam' Sutra which is very convenient. It is, however, not convenient in cases where the divisor is slightly over the base and consists of small digits. That is when the Paravartya method comes in handy. The smaller digits of the divisor are transposed i.e. '+' becomes '-' and vice versa, after which the division method becomes simple. Also, the Nikhilam method cannot be applied in algebraic division.

a) **To carry out algebraic division:**

For e.g :. Divide $12x^2 - 8x - 32$ by $(x - 2)$

$\underline{x - 2}$	$12x^2 - 8x - 32$	
$+2$	$\underline{\quad 24x + 32}$	
	$12x + 16$	0

We take x – 2 on the left side of the dividend, just below it we put down -2 with transposition i.e. +2 . Bring own the first term $12x^2$ of the dividend after dividing with x. Multiply the number 12x by 2 from the divisor, place under the second term, solve -8x + 24x = 16x and put this number down next to 12x, after dividing with x again. Multiply this number again by 2 and place under the constant term. Solve the same, the resulting number will be the remainder. Therefore, in the example above the Quotient(Q) = 12x +16 and the Remainder(R) = 0.

b) **To divide a number by a divisor above a base having small digits:**

For e.g. Divide 1234 by 112

112	1	2	3	4
-1 -2		-1	-2	
			-1	-2
	1	1	0	2

Therefore, Q = 11 and R = 02

Here the divisor 112 is close to base 100 and the deviation is +12. We take the divisor, as usual, to the left hand side of the dividend. Under it we take the transposed value of the deviation as -1 and -2 individually. Dividing, we bring down the first digit of the dividend as is and multiply each negative digit by this number as seen in the second row. We then solve for the second column and bring down the number next to the first Q digit and multiply this number by the transposed digits as seen in the third row. This covers all the digits of the dividend and we solve for the rest. We get 1102. To calculate the number of Q digits there will be in this division, we subtract the total digits of the divisor from that of the dividend and add 1 to the difference. Hence Q =11 and R = 02 is the solution.

Sutra 5 : " Shunyam Samyah Samucchaya"

Translation: '*When the Samucchayas are same, the Samucchaya is '0'*"

Application & Explanation:

'Samucchaya' means a lot of things but in the context of mathematics it means aggregate. This sutra is used for solving algebraic simple equations. The samucchaya is considered differently in different cases.

a) **Case 1**: If the common factor is the same, then the factor is zero.

e.g. in the equation $ax + bx = cx + dx$, x is the common factor and is the same in all terms, hence $x = 0$.

Another example: In $8(x - 3) = 6(x - 3)$, $(x - 3)$ is the common factor and same, therefore, $x - 3 = 0$, or $x = 3$.

b) **Case 2**: If the product of the independent terms are same, then the variable is zero.

e.g. in the equation $(x + 6)(x + 4) = (x - 8)(x - 3)$, the product of the independent terms on either side of the equation is 24, therefore $x = 0$.

c) **Case 3**: If the numerators are the same, then the sum of the denominators is zero.

e.g. in $\frac{6}{3x + 2} + \frac{6}{2x + 5} = 0$

the numerators are equal, so $3x + 2 + 2x + 5 = 0$
or $5x + 7 = 0$ or $x = -7/5$

d) **Case 4**: If the sums of the numerators and denominators are same, the sums are zero

e.g. in $\frac{6x + 3}{9x + 4} = \frac{9x + 4}{6x + 3} \Rightarrow \frac{6x + 3 + 9x + 4}{9x + 4 + 6x + 3} = \frac{15x + 7}{15x + 7}$,

so $15x + 7 = 0$ and $x = -7/15$

e) **Case 5**: Numerators being same, if sum of denominators are equal, sum is zero.

e.g. in $\frac{1}{x + 8} + \frac{1}{x + 4} = \frac{1}{x + 5} + \frac{1}{x + 7}$,

the sums of the denominators on both sides is $2x + 12$, so $2x + 12 = 0$.

Sutra 6: " Aanurupyeh Shunyamanyatam"

Translation: '*If one is in ratio, the other is zero*'

Application & Explanation:

This sutra is used in solving linear equations with two variables and states that if one variable term is in ratio to the independent term, then the other variable is zero.

For e.g. in the equations (i) $3x + 4y = 8$ and (ii) $x + 2y = 4$, the y term is in proportion to the independent term by 1 : 2, therefore $x = 0$ and $y = 2$.

Sutra 7 : "Sankalan Vyavakalanabhyam"

Translation : ' *By addition and by subtraction*'

Application & Explanation:

This sutra is used to solve linear equations whose coefficients of variables are interchanged. The equations are first added and then subtracted to arrive at two other equations, which are added again to arrive at the value of one variable.

e. g. in equations (i) $3x + 2y = 10$ and (ii) $2x + 3y = 5$; the coefficients of x and y are interchanged then,

(1) by addition, we get $3x + 2y + 2x + 3y = 10 + 5$ or $5x + 5y = 15$ or $x + y = 3$…(iii) and

(2) by subtraction we get $3x + 2y - 2x - 3y = 10 - 5$ or $x - y = 5$…(iv)

(3) by addition of (iii) & (iv), we get $x + y + x - y = 3 + 5$ or $2x = 8$ or $x = 4$ and $y = -1$

Sutra 8 : " Purnaapurnaabhyam"

Translation : ' *By completion or non-completion*'

Application & Explanation:

This sutra is used in **solving quadratic, cubic and bi-quadratic equations** by simplifying them to their nearest square, cube etc.

For e.g. (i) $x^2 + 3x + 2 = 0$ can be simplified to $(x + 2)^2$
Adding x + 2 on both sides, $x^2 + 3x + 2 + x + 2 = x + 2$
or $(x + 2)^2 = x + 2$;
Let $x + 2 = y$; So $y^2 = y$,
therefore, for $y = \{-1,0,1\}$ and $x = y - 2 = \{-3, -2, -1\}$.

Sutra 9: " Chalan Kalanaabhyam"

Translation: ' *By sequential motion or by calculus*'

Application & Explanation:

This sutra is used to solve quadratic equations and states that the differential is equal to the square root of the determinant. In the quadratic equation $ax^2 + bx + c = 0$, the differential is $2ax + b$ and the determinant $\Delta = b^2 - 4ac$ and $2ax + b = \pm\sqrt{b^2 - 4ac}$. Therefore,

$$x = \frac{-b \pm \sqrt{b^2 - 4ac}}{2a}$$

Sutra 10: " Yaavadunam"

Translation: '*By the deficiency*'

Application & Explanation :

This sutra is applied to work with numbers close to the base of 10, 10^2.....10^n. the deviation is calculated by subtracting the base from the number. If the number is higher than the base, the deviation/ deficiency is positive and vice versa. This formula is used to

a) Find the square of the number.

For e.g. to find $(98)^2$, we take base as 100, the deviation/deficiency as $98 - 100 = -2$ then

```
      98    -2
   x  98    -2
 (98 – 2) | 04  = 9604
```

taking the number on the left hand side and the deficiency on the right, we multiply the deficiencies and put the result on the right as a two digit number and add the number on the left to the deficiency of the other number and write the sum on the left side.

b) Multiply any two numbers close to the base.

For e.g. 999 x 985 can be solved thus

```
       999   -1
      x985   -15
   999-15 | 015 = 984015
```

Sutra 11: " Vyashti Samashti"

Translation :' *Specific and General*'

Application & Explanation :

The sutra is mainly used in **solving bi-quadratic equations** by conversion to simple quadratic equations

Example : To solve $(x+7)^4 + (x+5)^4 = 706$,
we take the average of the two terms $\frac{x+7+x+5}{2} = x+6$.
Let $u = x+6, \therefore x+7 = u+1 \; and \; x+5 = u-1$.
Substituting, $(u+1)^4 + (u-1)^4 = 706$
Solving, $u^4 + 4u^3 + 6u^2 + 4u + 1 + u^4 - 4u^3 + 6u^2 - 4u + 1 = 706$

$$\approx 2u^4 + 12u^2 - 704 = 0$$
$$\approx u^4 + 6u^2 - 352 = 0$$

Factoring,
$$\approx u^4 + 22u^2 - 16u^2 - 352 = 0$$
$$\approx u^2(u^2+22) - 16(u^2+22) = 0$$
$$\therefore u = \pm 4 \quad or \; u = \pm\sqrt{22}i$$
$$\therefore x = \{-2, -10, -6 \pm \sqrt{22}i\}$$

Sutra 12 : " Sheshanyankena Charamena"

Translation : '*The remainders by the last digit*'

Application & Explanation:

This sutra is used for **converting a vulgar fraction (having 7 as the denominator) to decimal form** with respect to the remainders.

Dividing 10 (adding a 0 to 1 to make the numerator greater than the denominator) by 7, we get the remainders as 3, 2, 6, 4, 5 and 1 after which the remainders repeat over again. When we multiply each remainder by the divisor 7, we get 21, 14, 42, 28, 35, 7 respectively.
Ignoring the left hand side digits, we simply put down the last digit (Charamanka) of each product and get

$$\frac{1}{7} = 0.\dot{1}4285\dot{7}$$

Sutra 13: " Sopaantya Dvayamantyam"

Translation: '*The ultimate and twice the penultimate*'

Application & Explanation:

The sutra is used to:

a) Multiply any number by 12

For e.g. To solve 7568 x 12, add a 0 on both sides of the number 075680. Starting from the left, add the ultimate digit and twice the penultimate(the digit before).

Solving,we get

$7 + 2(0) \mid 5 + 2(7) \mid 6 + 2(5) \mid 8 + 2(6) \mid 0 + 2(8)$
$= 7 \mid 19 \mid 16 \mid 20 \mid 16$
Keeping, the unit digit as 6 and carrying 1, we continue adding from right to left; so 7568 x12 = 90816

b) Solve simple equations whose factors of denominators are in Arithmetic Progression.

Example: The equation:

$$\frac{1}{(x+3)(x+4)}+\frac{1}{(x+3)(x+5)}=\frac{1}{(x+3)(x+6)}+\frac{1}{(x+4)(x+5)}$$

Can be solved using the sutra, where the ultimate term is (x + 6) and the penultimate term is (x + 5),
by adding (x +6) + 2(x +5) = 0 $\approx 3x = -11$
So , $x = \frac{-11}{3}$

Sutra 14: " Ekanyunena Purvena"

Translation : '*By one less than the previous*'

Application & Explanation :

This sutra seems to be the opposite of the first sutra ' By one more than the previous one'. It is used to multiply any number by a multiplier that has only 9s as digits viz. 9, 99, 999 etc. To get a better understanding, let us look at the 9 times table below:

1 x 9 =	**0**	**9**
2 x 9 =	**1**	**8**
3 x 9 =	**2**	**7**
4 x 9 =	**3**	**6**
5 x 9 =	**4**	**5**
6 x 9 =	**5**	**4**
7 x 9 =	**6**	**3**
8 x 9 =	**7**	**2**
9 x 9 =	**8**	**1**
10 x 9 =	**9**	**0**

Here, we observe that for the single digit multiplier, the left digit of the product is 1 less than the multiplicand and the right side digit of the product is a complement of the left side digit from 9. This principle holds the same for 2 digit, 3 digit etc. multipliers There are three conditions taken into consideration here:

a) When the number of digits in the multiplicand and the multiplier are equal:

Example: 3243 x 9999

Here the number of digits in the multiplicand is 4 and there are four 9's in the multiplier. As explained above, deduct 1 from the multiplicand i.e. 3243 – 1 =3242. This gives us the left hand side digits of the product. To find the right hand side digits, take the complements from 9 for each left hand side digit i.e. 6757

$\therefore 3243 \times 9999 = 32436757$

b) When the number of digits in the multiplicand are lesser than those of the multiplier.

Example: 7865 x 99999

In this case, add a 0 before the multiplicand to equate the number of digits and continue as above. 07865 – 1 = 07864 for the left side and 92135 for the right hand side. Hence, the product is 786492135.

c) When the digits in the multiplicand are greater than the multiplier

Example: 12345 x 999

This problem is solved slightly differently.

Step 1: Divide the multiplicand with a vertical line having the right hand side digits the same as the multiplier i.e. 12 | 345 x 999

Step 2: Add 1 to the number on the left hand and side and subtract from the number in the right hand side i.e. 12 | 345 – (12 + 1) = 12332. This is the number for the left hand side of the product.

Step 3: to find the right hand side of the product, use the Nikhilam method 'all from 9, last from 10' and find the complement of the right hand side part of the multiplicand i.e. 345 = 655.Hence the product = 12332655

Sutra 15 : " Gunitasamuchhayah"

Translation: '*Product of the sum*'

Application & Explanation:

This sutra is used with the 13th sub-sutra 'Samuchhaya Gunitah' in connection with solving quadratic, cubic and biquadratic equations for the purpose of checking the correctness of the answers obtained from their multiplication, division and factorisation. In this context, the principle held is – ' the product of the sum of the coefficients in the factors is equal to the sum of the coefficients in the product'

Example: (x + 4)(x +5) = $x^2 + 9x + 20$

Product of the sum of the coefficients in the factors= (1 +4)(1 +5) =30
Sum of coefficients in the product = 1 + 9 + 20 = 30. Hence verified that factorisation is correct.

Sutra 16 : " Gunakasamucchayah"

Translation: '*All the multipliers or set of multipliers*'

Application & Explanation:

This sutra is useful in checking the solving of quadratic equations by 'chalana kalanabhyam' or calculus method. The differential of the quadratic expression should be the sum of the factors.

Example: if $ax^2 + bx + c = (x + d)(x + e), then\ 2ax + b = (x + d)(x + e)$

e.g. $x^2 + 5x + 4 = (x + 4)(x + 1)\ \ or\ 2x + 5 = x + 4 + x + 1$

$2x + 5 = 2x + 5$. Hence, verified.

B.THE UPASUTRAS

The upasutras or corollaries are useful in supporting the sutras in special cases with additional properties to make calculations easy and quick. There are 13 Upasutras mentioned.

Upasutra 1: "Aanurupyena"

Translation: '*Proportionately*'

Application & Explanation:

This Upasutra is a corollary to the first sutra to continue calculations proportionately after applying 'ekaadhikena' and resembles the second sutra 'nikhilam'. It is used:

a) **To multiply numbers not close to their bases by using sub-bases:**

Example: To solve 46 x 48 we can take the base as 100 and the nearest sub-base as 50. The deviations of the two numbers from 50 will be -4 and -2 respectively. Solving as in Nikhilam method, we get the product of the deviations as -4 x -2 = 08 which is the right hand side of the product. For the left hand side, we solve 46 + (-2) or 48 + (-4) = 44. Since sub-base 50 $=\frac{100}{2}$, we divide this number by 2 and get 22. Hence product is 2208.

b) **For finding cubes of numbers**:

Example: to find $(12)^3$, we take the number as a ratio 1:2. To solve, we take 4 spaces divided into 2 parts by a vertical line.
Step 1: In the first space, we write the cube of the digit in the tens place. In this case it will be 1.

Step 2: In the last or fourth space we write down the cube of the units digit, in this case 8.
Step 3: By observation of the ratio 1:2, the second space will have the number 2 and the third place will be 4, proportionately (1:2 | 4:8).
Step 4: We then double the number in the second and third place and add them to the same number i.e. 1 | 2 + 2(2) | 4 + 2(4) |8 = 1 | 6 | 12 | 8. Since there can be only 1 digit in each space, the 1 in 12 will carried over to the second space giving us the cube =1728.

Upasutra 2: "Shishyateh Sheshasangyah"

Translation: '*The remainder remains constant*'

Application & Explanation:

This upasutra is used while dividing large numbers with large divisors

.

Example: 1063 ÷ 27. 27 has 3 and 9 as factors. 9 : 27 = 1 : 3 & 3 : 9 = 1 : 3.

The first step is to divide 1063 by 9 (Quotient(Q) = 118, Remainder(R) = 1) and then divide 118 by 3 where we get Q =39 and R = 1.

$\therefore 1063 \div 27 = 39\left(\frac{1}{3} + \frac{1}{27}\right) = \mathrm{Q} = 39, \mathrm{R} = \frac{10}{27}$ or 10.

Upasutra 3: "Aadhyamaadhyeh Naantyamantyena"

Translation: '*The first by the first and the last by the last*'

Application & Explanation:

Used to solve quadratic equations by factorisation method, this upasutra is a shortcut to finding the factors.

Example: In $5x^2 + 12x + 4 = 5x^2 + 10x + 2x + 4$, the coefficients are in the ratio 1 : 2 so the first factor is $(x + 2)$. To get the second factor, we divide the first term of the equation by the first term of the factor $\frac{5x^2}{x} = 5x$ and the last term of the equation by the second term of the factor $\frac{4}{2} = 2$. $\therefore$ the second factor is (5x + 2) and the solution = (x + 2)(5x + 2).

Upasutra 4: "Kevalyeh Saptakam Gunayat"

Translation: ' *For 7 multiplicand is 143*'

Application & Explanation:

To understand this upasutra, we must take a look at the number 7. When we convert a fraction with 7 as its denominator we get a cyclic repetitive number.

As shown before $\frac{1}{7} = 0.14285\dot{7}$. When we observe this decimal we get 142857 = 143 x 999. This makes the answer easier to remember that 'for division by 7 the multiplicand is 143'. This is considered cyclic as

$\frac{2}{7} = 0.285714$, $\frac{3}{7} = 0.428571$, $\frac{4}{7} = 0.571428$ etc. the same digits are repeated.

Upasutra 5: "Veshtanam"

Translation: '*By osculation*'

Application & Explanation:

To check for divisibility of a number by a certain divisor, this upasutra comes in handy. The method employed is to find the positive (P) osculator (*Veshtana*) – the '*Ekadhika*' and negative (Q) osculator – the '*Viparita*' of the divisor.

To find P, we multiply the divisor by the smallest number to get a product having 9 as the unit digit. We then add 1(Ekadhikena) and divide by 10, to get the value of P. Algebraically, if 'n' is the divisor, 'k' is the smallest multiplier, then P = (nk +1)/10 is the positive osculator.

To find Q, we multiply the divisor 'n' by the smallest number 'k' to get a product having 1 as the unit digit. We then subtract 1 from the product and divide by 10 to get Q. Q = (nk – 1)/10 is the negative osculator. Another important point to remember is that n = P + Q.

To check for divisibility, we need to select the appropriate osculator and keep multiplying the unit digit of the dividend and adding or subtracting from the rest of the number. We continue in this manner till all digits of the dividend are covered. If the final answer is 0 or a multiple of the divisor, the dividend is divisible by the divisor.

Example: Is 123459 divisible by 7?

The first step is to find the osculators. P =7(7) +1/10 = 5 and Q = $\bar{2}$. Since both osculators are small numbers, we can use either to check for divisibility in the following way:

Using P, 12345~~9~~ x 5

+45

1239~~0~~ x5

+45

168 x 5

+40

56 (8 * 7)

Using Q, $\bar{1}2\bar{3}4\bar{5}9 \times 2$

(2*9 -5 = 13) x 2

(2*3 -1 + 4 = 9) x 2

(2*9 -0 +(-3) = 15) x 2

(2*5 -1 + 2 = 11) x 2

(2*1 -1 +(-1) = 0)

Therefore, 123459 is divisible by 7.

Upasutra 6: " Yaavadunam Taavadunam"

Translation: ' *Lessen by the deficiency*'

Application & Explanation:

This upasutra is useful in finding cubes of numbers close to their bases. The method employed is to make 3 spaces for the product with the last two spaces having same number of digits as the 0s in the base.

The third place will contain the cube of the deviation from the base. The first place will have the sum of the number and twice the deviation. The second place will be the product of the deviation of the number in the first place with the original deviation. The entire product is obtained after carrying over excess digits.

Example: Find $(104)^3$

The base for the above number = 100, the deviation(d) = 104 – 100 = 4.

The third space number will be $4^3 = 64$
The first space number = 104 + 2(4) = 112. The new deviation(D) will be 112 – 100 = 12.
The second space number = D x d = 12 x 4 = 48.
Hence, $(104)^3 = 1124864$.

Upasutra 7: " Yaavadunam Taavadunikritya Varga Cha Yojayet"

Translation: ' *Whatever the deficiency, lessen by that amount and set up the square of the deficiency*'.

Application & Explanation:

The above upasutra is used in finding squares of numbers close to their base.

Example: Find $(98)^2$

The number is close to the base 100 and deviation is 98 – 100 = -2. Then, lessening the number by deviation we get 96 and setting up the square of the deficiency = $(-2)^2 = 04$.
We add a 0 before the 4 to get two digits as required by the number of 0s in the base.

$$\therefore (98)^2 = 98 + (-2) \mid (-2)^2 = 9604$$

Upasutra 8: "Antyayordashakepi"

Translation: '*Last totalling as 10*'

Application & Explanation:

Used to multiply two numbers whose end digits add up to 10 or powers of 10 and the first digits are same. The product is arrived at by multiplying the end digits and writing the number to the right with requisite number of digits and multiplying the first digit by one more than itself.

Example: 56 x 54 meets the requirement having the sum of the units digits as 10 and the tens place digit being the same. The product = 5 x (5 + 1) | 6 x 4 = 30 | 24 = 3024.

Upasutra 9: " Antyayoreva"

Translation: ' *Only the last terms*'.

Application & Explanation:

This upasutra is used in

a) Solving algebraic equations:

(i) **Case 1**: Equations where the numerator and denominator on the left hand side, barring the independent terms, are in the same ratio as the entire numerator and denominator on the right hand side

Example:

$$\frac{x^2+4x+6}{x^2+5x+8}=\frac{x+4}{x+5}$$

On the left hand side, ignoring the independent terms we get

$$\frac{x^2+4x}{x^2+5x}=\frac{x(x+4)}{x(x+5)}=\frac{x+4}{x+5}$$

LHS=RHS. Taking the independent terms, we solve for

$$\frac{x+4}{x+5}=\frac{6}{8} => 8x+32=6x+30 => x=\ -1$$

(ii) **Case 2**: If the factors of the denominator are in Arithmetic Progression(A.P) or related to each other in a special manner, the sum of the series will have the numerator as the sum of all numerators and the denominator as the product of the two ends.

Example:

$$\frac{1}{(x+1)(x+2}+\frac{1}{(x+2)(x+3)}+\frac{1}{(x+3)(x+4)}$$

The solution will have the numerator = sum of all numerators = 3 and the denominator = product of the two end factors = (x + 1)(x+4)

$$\frac{3}{(x+1)(x+4)}=\frac{3}{x^2+5x+4}$$

(iii) **Case 3**: Equations where the numerator as the difference of the binomials of the factors of its denominator are solved as a sum of series having the numerator as the sum of all numerators and the denominator as the product of the two end factors.

Example:

$$\frac{a-b}{(x+a)(x+b)}+\frac{b-c}{(x+b)(x+c)}+\frac{c-d}{(x+c)(x+d)}$$

$$=\frac{a-b+b-c+c-d}{(x+a)(x+d)}=\frac{a-d}{(x+a)(x+d)}$$

b) **Multiplying with 11,111,1111..**and so on. When multiplying by 11, 111 1111… a few things have to be considered:

(i) [(The total number of digits in the multiplicand and multiplier) – 1] will be the least number of digits in the product.

(ii) Multiplication with 11, 111 etc. is a series of multiple additions of the digits of the multiplicand. The number of digits to be added will depend on the number of digits in the multiplier. For e.g. when multiplying with 11, 2 digits will be added, if by 111, then 3 digits maximum and so forth.

(iii) The first (if it does not precede a carrying number) and last digits of the multiplicand will remain the same.

Example: a) 1345 x 11 will have a minimum of (6 -1= 5) digits. We can divide the product into 5 spaces. The first space will contain the first digit number i.e. 1, the second space will be 1 +3 =4, the third will be 3 +4 = 7, the fourth will have 4 + 5 = 9 and the last space will contain the last digit of the multiplicand i.e. 5. Therefore the product = 14795
Example: b) 1345 x 111 = 1 | 1 +3 | **1 + 3 + 4** | 3 + 4 + 5 | 4 + 5 | 5 = 1 | 4 | 8 | 12 | 9 | 5. (max no. of digits reached)

Since each space can have only one digit, then the fourth space number 12 will be written as 2 and 1 will be carried over to the third space. Hence, 1345 x 111 = 149295. In the third and fourth space the maximum number of digits to be added are 3, hence the third space will have the first 3 digits added up and the fourth will have the next 3 digits added up.

Upasutra 10: " Samucchaya Gunita"

Translation: ' *The sum of the products*'

Application & Explanation:

This upasutra is applied together with the Sutra 15 and Upasutra 13 in solving algebraic equations as explained in the Sutra where the product of the sum of the coefficients of the factors is equal to the sum of the coefficients of the product.

Upasutra 11: " Lopasthapanabhyam"

Translation: ' *By alternate elimination and retention*'

Application & Explanation:

Factorising harder quadratic equations is easily done by applying this upasutra.

Example: Factorise $2x^2 + 6y^2 + 3z^2 + 7xy + 11yz + 7zx$. There are 3 variables x, y, z.

Then by first elimination, let y = 0 => $2x^2 + 0 + 3z^2 + 0 + 0 + 7zx$ => $2x^2 + 6zx + zx + 3z^2$ => $2x(x + 3z) + z(x + 3z)$ => $(x + 3z)(2x + z)$.

Keeping the factors thus obtained now let z =0 => $2x^2 + 6y^2 + 0 + 7xy + 0 + 0$ => $2x^2 + 4xy + 3xy + 6y^2$ => $2x(x + 2y) + 3y(x + 2y)$ => $(x + 2y)(2x + 3y)$

Comparing the two set of factors, we can see that each has x and 2x that are same, retaining this we have the factors as $\boldsymbol{(x + 2y + 3z)(2x + 3y + z)}$

Upasutra 12: " Vilokanam"

Translation: ' *By observation*'

Application & Explanation:

Since most of the problems are calculated mentally in Vedic Mathematics, observation is very important in solving the same. This Upasutra is used to:

a) **Find the square root of a perfect square:** let us look at the following table :

$1^2 =$	1	$6^2 =$	36
$2^2 =$	4	$7^2 =$	49
$3^2 =$	9	$8^2 =$	64
$4^2 =$	16	$9^2 =$	81
$5^2 =$	25	$10^2 =$	100

In this table we can see that (i) perfect squares do not end with 2, 3, 7 and 8. (ii) Squares ending with 1, can have square root ending with either 1 or 9, ending with 4, will have 2 or 8, ending with 9 will have 3 or 7, ending with 6 will have either 4 or 6 and finally ending with 5 will have a square root ending with 5.

Example: Find $\sqrt{4489}$.

The first step is to group the numbers in two from the right hand side. Here we have 44 and 89. This means that there will be two digits in the answer.

Next, we see that the square ends in 9. We can deduce that the square root will end in either 3 or 7.

Now we see that the nearest perfect square number to 44 is 36 = 62. So the square root can be either 63 or 67.

To select the correct number we can take the square of 65(average of 63 and 69) = 4225. This number is smaller than 4489. Therefore we take the larger number i.e. 67. ∴ $\mathbf{\sqrt{4489}}$ = **67**

b) **Find the cube root of a perfect cube**: In the table below, we can see that cubes ending with 1, 4, 5, 6 and 9 will have corresponding cube roots ending in 1, 4, 5, 6 and 9. Cubes ending with 8 will have its cube root ending with 2 and vice versa and cubes ending with 7 will have cube root ending with 3 and vice versa.

$1^3 =$	1	$6^3 =$	216
$2^3 =$	8	$7^3 =$	343
$3^3 =$	27	$8^3 =$	512
$4^3 =$	64	$9^3 =$	729
$5^3 =$	125	$10^3 =$	1000

To find the cube root of a perfect cube we group the digits in 3s from the right hand side.

Example: Find $\sqrt[3]{19683}$ .We get two groups viz. 19 and 683. The last digit of the cube is 3. Hence the cube root will have 7 as its end digit. The closest cube to 19 is $2^3 = 8$. So our first digit is 2 and the cube root is thus 27.∴ $\boldsymbol{\sqrt[3]{19683} = 27}$

c) **To solve simple algebraic equations:** Example: Solve:

$$x + \frac{1}{x} = \frac{5}{2} \;\; => \frac{5}{2} = 2 + \frac{1}{2} \;\; => \therefore x + \frac{1}{x} = 2 + \frac{1}{2}$$

So x = $\{2, \frac{1}{2}\}$

d) **For addition:** this concept encourages the student to solve addition problems from left to right. To do this there are some basic rules

(i) End number concept: when adding two numbers, if the sum is in two digits, in other words if the numbers are carrying numbers the addition of the previous number is increased by 1.

(ii) 9's combination exception- where the sum of 9 appears in the middle digits, and the following pair of digits are carrying numbers then we the sum becomes 0 and the previous pair sum increases by 1. Otherwise the sum can be written as 9.

Example: Add: (i) 745 + 832 = 1577 calculation to be done from leftmost pair of digits. (ii) 268 + 634 = 902. Since the middle digits add up to 9 and the sum of the next pair of digits is 12(a carrying number), we write the last digit of the sum as the end number of 12 i.e. 2, 6 + 3 +1 =10, writing down the end number here as 0 we add 1 to the sum of the first pair of digits which becomes 9.

Upasutra 13: " Gunita Samucchayaha Samucchaya Gunitaha"

Translation: ' *The product of the sums is the sum of the products*'

Application & Explanation:

This upasutra has been discussed in Sutra 15.

SPECIAL METHODS OR VIDHIS

Apart from the 16 Sutras and 13 Upasutras, there are certain special formulae and methods or 'vidhis' in Vedic mathematics. These may also be termed as special Upasutras. A brief explanation has been given here and will be discussed, in more details, in the following chapters of this book.

I. SUDHA VIDHI

This is used to add multiple numbers by calling out the end number digit of the sum and placing a dot for every carrying number. The number of dots represent the total of 10s to carry over. This is also called the 'Dot Method' of addition

Example: Add 3 4 5
2 7˙4
˙4 5 6˙
+ 5 6˙5˙
1640

II. VINCULUM VIDHI

A vinculum number is one having a combination of positive and negative digits. This is useful to carry out the mathematical operations when presented with numbers having digits equal to or greater than 5. It allows for simplification in solving problems.

A vinculum number is written as having a negative sign over the negative digit. For e.g. $4\bar{3}$ is a vinculum number where 4 is positive and 3 is negative. To convert these numbers we have to review the number place value system where a number 1234 = 1000 + 200 + 30 + 4. Similarly, $4\bar{3}$ can be written as 40 + (- 3) = 37.

To convert a number into a vinculum number, say 49, take the complement of the units digit from 10, write this complement as a negative number and add 1 to the tens place digit. The number 49 = $5\bar{1}$ (50 – 1 = 49) as a vinculum number. To convert a vinculum number, we again take the complement of the negative number from10 and reduce the tens place number by 1. If there are more than one negative numbers in a row we use the Nikhilam method of finding the complements from 9 for all negative numbers and the last from 10.

This method is used in various ways

1.) **Easy subtraction:** the conventional Vilokanam method of end digits, carrying numbers and 9's exception is abandoned in this method. The number from which another number is to be subtracted is the 'minuend' and the number to be subtracted is called the 'subtrahend'. Starting from the left, subtract each subtrahend digit from the corresponding minuend digit. If the subtrahend digit is greater than the minuend digit, subtract the minuend from the subtrahend and write it as a negative number with a bar on it. Continue in this manner till all digits of the subtrahend have been used. The answer thus obtained will give us a combination of positive and negative digits. Using the conversion method convert all vinculum numbers to positive numbers using the nikhilam sutra

Example:

$$\begin{array}{r} 4\,4\,2\,7\,5 \\ \underline{-3\,2\,8\,9\,4} \\ 1\,1\,3\,8\,1 \\ \text{(a)} \end{array} \qquad \begin{array}{r} 4\,4\,2\,7\,5 \\ \underline{-\,3\,2\,8\,9\,4} \\ 1\,2\,\overline{6\,2}\,1 \\ \text{(b)} \end{array} \qquad \begin{array}{r} 4\,4\,2\,7\,5 \\ \underline{+\overline{3\,2\,8\,9\,4}} \\ 1\,2\,\overline{6\,2}\,1 = 1\,1\,3\,8\,1 \\ \text{(c)} \end{array}$$

In the example above, (a) has been done in the conventional observation method. The second method has been explained above. The third method is to change the ' – ' sign to ' + ' and take the entire subtrahend as vinculum numbers. This method allows for faster and more accurate calculations.

2.) **In multiplication:** This application can be better explained with an example.

Multiply 222 x 178. Since 7 and 8 are large numbers and will involve large products, we take the vinculum number of 178 which is $2\bar{2}\bar{2}$. Therefore, multiplying 222 x $2\bar{2}\bar{2}$ by the vertically and crosswise method, we get the product as $40\overline{484}$ = **39516.**

Hence large numbers can be multiplied very easily and accurately b this method.

3.) **In division**: by the 'Flag' method. This method is explained in this chapter itself.

To understand the concept let us see an example.

Divide 1448 by 29. In the flag division method, the divisor is grouped into the main divisor and the modified multiplier. In this case, the main divisor will be 2 and the modified multiplier will be 9. Since 9 > 5, we can take the vinculum number of 29 which is $3\bar{1}$.

Flag digit	$\bar{1}$				
Main divisor | Dividend	29 3	**1**	**4**	**4**	**8**
Dividend with remainder			14	24	18
Flag subtrahend			0	-(4)	- (-9)
Modified dividend			14	28	**27**
Divisor x quotient		0	12	27	
Quotient		**0**	**4**	**9**	

In the above division, 3 is the main divisor, $\bar{1}$ is the flag digit or modified multiplier. The dividend will be written next to the divisor with a separate group for the last digit. This number is for the remainder. Since there is a single flag digit, we take only the last digit of the dividend.

Dividing by 3, we get our first quotient as 4 and remainder as 2. This 2 along with the next digit of the dividend i.e. 4 will give us a new dividend which is 24. We then multiply the quotient 4 with the flag digit. The product will be -4. This is subtracted from the new dividend 24 – (-4) = 28. Therefore, 28 is the modified dividend to be further divided by 3. The next quotient digit will be 9 giving the product as 27 and remainder as 1. The new dividend is in the remainder portion. Multiplying 9 with the flag digit we get -9 and subtracting this from the new dividend, we get 18 – (-9) = 27.

This number is the remainder. Hence $\mathbf{448 \div 29 = 49\frac{27}{29}}$.

III. BEEJANK VIDHI

This method is also called '*Navashesh*' method or Digital Root (DR) method or Digital Sum (DS) method. It is useful for checking of answers obtained while carrying out mathematical operations on numbers.

The DR or DS is obtained by adding all the digits of a number till 1 digit remains. DR/ DS cannot be a multiple digit number.

The DR, also, cannot be a negative number. If we obtain a negative solution, we simply add by 9 and get the positive true DR.

While adding the digits we can ignore all 9s and numbers adding up to 9. This will not affect the DR value. If, however, we get a 0 on addition, we take the DR as 9. If a number is multiplied by 9, the DR will always be a 9. Alternately, if the DR of a number is 9, the number is divisible by 9.

Checking answers of operations is done by finding the DR of all numbers in use and treating the DRs to the same operation. Hence,

(i) For Addition: The DRs of the numbers to be added are added and compared to the DR of the sum obtained from addition. If these are same then the calculations are correct. This will hold true only if there is no error in placing the digits of the solution correctly i.e. no error in writing the answer in the correct form, since the same digits placed wrongly, will still give us the same DR but the sum could be wrong.

Example: Add 456 +467+334. The sum = 1257. The DR of 456 =6, DR of 467= 8, DR of 334 = 1 and DR of the sum = 6. Adding the first 3 DRs we get 6 + 8 + 1 = 6 = DR of the sum. Hence the addition is correct.

(ii) For Subtraction: The DR of the minuend and of the subtrahend are subtracted. If the subtraction is a negative number, a 9 is added to get the real positive value. This subtraction is compared to the DR of the answer of the actual subtraction.

Example: Subtract 12345 – 6544. The answer = 5801. DR of 12345 = 6, DR of 6544 = 1 and DR of the subtraction = 5. Subtracting the first 2 DRs we get 6 – 1 = 5 = DR of the subtraction. Therefore, the subtraction is correct.

(iii) For Multiplication: The DR of the multiplicand is multiplied by the DR of the multiplier to get the product. DR of the actual product should be the same as this product.
Example: 18 x 12 = 216. DR (18) x DR (12) = DR (216).
9 x 3 = 9. ≈ 27 = 9. ≈2 + 7 = 9. This statement is true. Hence, the multiplication is correct.

(iv) For Division: To check for division, we calculate the DRs of the Dividend (M), Divisor (D), Quotient (Q) and Remainder (R). Then we use the formula: **DR (M) = [DR (D) x DR(Q) + DR(R)]**

Example: 1448 ÷ 29 = 49 with a remainder of 27.
Here, M = 1448, D = 29, Q = 49 and R = 27. Therefore, DR(M)= 8, DR(D) = 2, DR (Q) = 4 and DR(R) =9. Checking with the formula,8 = (2 x 4) + 9 = 8+9 = 8. The division is correct.

IV. DHVAJANK VIDHI

This is also called the 'Flag' method and is used for division. In this 'vidhi' or method, the divisor is separated into two groups. The first group from the divisor is called the '**Mukhyank**' or main divisor. The second part, the 'Dhvajank' or modified multiplier, is written above and to the right of the mukhyank, resembling a flag. For example, if we have a divisor as 42, we take 4 as the mukhyank and 2 as the dhvajank and it will be written as :

Dhvajank	2|	
Mukhyank	4 |	Dividend

Depending upon the number of digits in the flag, the dividend will be grouped, from the right with just as many digits to represent the remainder portion of the division method.

The division is carried out by dividing each digit, from the left by the mukhyank. The remainder of each division is carried to the next digit of the dividend as the new dividend, just like in the conventional method of division.

The difference here is that the new dividend is subjected to subtraction of the product of the flag digit with the quotient from it. This subtraction will give us the modified dividend which will once again be divided by the mukhyank and will continue till all the digits of the dividend are used up to give us the final quotient and remainder.

We can divide the remainder further to get the solution as a decimal number.

Example: 38982 ÷ 73

Flag digit	3					
Main divisor | Dividend	7	3	8	9	8	2
Dividend with remainder			38	39	38	12
Flag subtrahend			0	-15	-9	-12
Modified dividend			38	24	29	**0**
Divisor x quotient		0	35	21	28	
Quotient		**0**	**5**	**3**	**4**	

In this division,

(i) We group the divisor 73 as 7 being the mukhyank or main divisor and 3 being the dhvajank or modified multiplier.

(ii) Since there is only one digit in the flag, we will group the dividend 38982 by placing a line before the last digit to denote the remainder portion. For e.g. 3898 | 2

(iii) Start dividing the number by the mukhyank. The first quotient number will be 5 as we cannot divide 3 by 7 so we take 38 as the first dividend. This division gives us a remainder of 3. This is taken to the next dividend digit and the new dividend will be 39.

(iv) Subtract the product of the flag digit and the first quotient i.e. 3 x 5 =15, from 39,and we get 24 as the modified dividend. Now we proceed to divide this number by 7. The quotient will now be 3 and the remainder will be 3. As before, the new dividend 38 – the flag subtrahend 9 (3 x 3) will give us the modified dividend as 29.

(v) Dividing 29 by 7, the quotient will be 4 and remainder will be 1. The new dividend in the remainder portion of the dividend will be 12 and the modified one will be 12 – (4 x 3) =0. Hence 38982 ÷ 73 = 534 with remainder as 0. So, Q = 534 and R = 0.

There can be more than 1 digit in the flag as well as vinculum numbers. The method of division, in these cases is discussed in the Division chapter of this book.

V. DVANDVA YOG VIDHI

This method is also called the 'Duplex' method. It is used in finding squares of any numbers as well as in finding the square root of perfect squares. Before we get into the application, let us understand the basic concept of this method. Finding duplex of numbers is as follows:

Duplex(D) of a single digit(a) is its square i.e. $D(a) = a^2$
Duplex of a 2 digit number(ab) : $D(ab) = 2 \times a \times b = 2ab$
Duplex of a 3 digit number(abc) : $D(abc) = 2ac + b^2$
Duplex of a 4 digit number(abcd) : $D(abcd) = 2ad + 2bc$
Duplex of a 5 digit number (abcde): $D(abcde) = 2ae + 2bd + c^2$.

On observation, we see that if there are two digits in a number then the duplex of the two digits is twice their product, in case of a 3 digit number the duplex of the three digits is twice the product of the first and last digit added to the square of the middle digit and so on.

-This makes for **easy calculation of the square of any number**.
For e.g. find (i)13^2 and (ii) 145^2

(i) In this first problem, we can write $13^2 = D(1) | D(13) | D(3) = 1^2 | 2 \times 1 \times 3 | 3^2 = 1 | 6 | 9$. Therefore, $\mathbf{13^2 = 169}$.

(ii) 145^2 = D(1) | D(14) | D(145) | D(45) | D(5) = 1^2 | 2 x 1 x 4 | 2 x 1 x 5 + 4^2 | 2 x 4 x 5 | 5^2 = 1 | 8 | 26 | 40 | 25.

Applying a balancing rule, starting from the right, we write down the unit digit of each part and carry over the rest to the left and continue in this way so that there is only 1 digit in each part of the multiplication.
Hence 1 | 8 | 26 | 40 | 25 = 2 | 1 | 0 | 2 | 5. Therefore **145^2 = 21025.**

-The duplex method is also used in **finding the square roots of a perfect square.** Let us take the examples from above as : Find (i)$\sqrt{169}$ and (ii) $\sqrt{21025}$

(i) The first step to finding the square root is to group the number in twos from the right. Then 169 will be 1 & 69 after grouping. This grouping also helps in determining the number of digits (n) in the square root. So the number of digits in the square root of 169 will be 2. Look at the following division:

	(a^2)		
	1	$^{0}6$	$^{0}9$
		0	-09 (- D(3))
(2a)		06	
2	1	06	
	1	**3.**	**0**
	(a)	(b)	

The first step after grouping is to place the first group of numbers in the left and draw a separating line to the write for the rest of the numbers. Here the number in the first group is 1 and the square root of 1 is 1. We bring this number down and write it as the first digit of the square root. This number is doubled and written to the left of the first dividing line. This will be the divisor now. Since there is no remainder in the first part of the division we write a 0 a little above and to the left of the next digit. Therefore the new dividend is 06. 2 will divide 06 giving us a quotient of 3 and 0 as the remainder. We write this as 09 for the next dividend. This 09, however, is not the actual dividend. We have to subtract the duplex of the last quotient number i.e. 3 from this dividend. Hence 09 – D(3) = 09 – 3^2 = 0. Since the dividend is 0 there can be no further division. As there are 2 digits in the square root, the answer to $\sqrt{169} = 13$.

(ii) Grouping 21025 we have 3 groups (2, 10, 25) so n =3, the first group will have 2 in the first part of the division.

	2	$^{1}1$	$^{3}0$	$^{4}2$	$^{2}5$	
		0	-16	-40	-25	
		11	14	2	0	
2	1	8	10	0	0	
	1		4	5 .	0	
			-D(4)	-D(45)		-D(450)

In the above division, as before, the first dividend number is 2 and the nearest perfect square to 2(a^2) is 1. We will take the first quotient as 1(a) and remainder as 1. Doubling the quotient we get 2(2a) as the divisor. The next dividend is 11 which on dividing by 2 will give us Q = 5(b) and R = 1, the next dividend will be 10 and if we subtract D(5) = 25 from it, we will get a negative solution. So we reduce the quotient to 4 and get 30 as the dividend. Subtracting D(4) = 16, the new dividend will be 14. Again by observation we see that the dividend with a quotient 7 or 6 will be 02 or 22 and the next subtrahend will be D (47) = 56 or D(46) = 48 and give us a negative answer. If we take the quotient as 5, the dividend will be 42 and the subtrahend will be D(45) = 40 giving us the new dividend as 2. Instead of 1 , if we take 0 as the next quotient we will get the next dividend as 25 and the subtrahend for this dividend will be D(450) = 25. The dividend is 0 now and no further digits are left to be divided. So our solution is $\sqrt{21025} = 145$.

THE VEDIC NUMERICAL CODE

During the vedic period, the mathematicians did not use figures to denote numbers. Instead of numbers the letters of the Devnagari script were used. This can be seen even in the mathematical formulae given as words istead of numbers. The reason behind such usage was not to confuse the student but make it easier for him to remember and recall. The literary works of all sciences in the vedas are in the verse form. The students would learn and recite these much more easily.

The key to understanding numbers from verse is given in the following form: ' Kaa di nava, ta di nava, Paa di panchak, yaadyashtaka and Kshah shunyam, which translated means

a) ka and the following 8 letters
b) ta and the following 8 letters
c) paa and the following 4 letters
d) yaa and the following 7 letters and
e) Ksha for 0

This can be shown thus:

1	Ka,	ta,	paa	& yaa
2	Kha,	tha,	pha,	& ra
3	Ga,	da,	ba	& la
4	Gha,	dha,	bha	& va
5	Gna,	na,	ma	& sa
6	Cha,	ta		& sha
7	Chha,	tha		& sa
8	Ja	da		& ha
9	Jha	dha		
0	Ksha			

PART II

VEDIC ARITHMETIC

Chapter 1

YOJANAM / ADDITION

Addition is the process by which two or more numbers are assimilated into one large number. There are various ways or methods to do so. Before we begin, however, there are some exercises that the students may practice for faster calculations and increased concentration power.

1. Since Vedic mathematics is more a mental method of doing math problems, it is important that the student call out numbers 1 to 100 slowly, at first and then pick up speed and accuracy.
2. Once the speed is achieved, the student then should call out the numbers backwards like 100, 99, 98, 97…to 1. As before, practice for speed and accuracy.
3. The next exercises are to skip 1, 2 3 4..etc numbers and call out from 1 to 100 like 1, 3, 5, 7….99 & 100 and do the same in reverse. The more speed the student achieves the more the concentration increases and, with it, the accuracy.

Before we proceed with the various operations of arithmetic, we need to under stand a concept called :

The balancing rule: This is the calculations carried out when using mathematical operations on numbers by grouping the various digits of the solution into a number of parts. Then starting from the right, retaining the required number of digits for that part, carry over any extra digit/s to the next part to the left of it. This continues till all the parts are 'balanced' out to get the solution.

For example:

Multiplying 345 x 478 = 12 | 37 | 72 | 67 | 40 = 164910

The above multiplication is done by the Urdhva Triyagbhyam Sutra (explained in a later chapter). Multiplying from left to right, each step results in the 5 solutions which are held in the 5 parts above. The solution is now in the 'balancing' and each part from the second part to the last part is to have only 1 digit place. The balancing will be done by :

- Keeping 0 from 40, in the last part and carrying the extra digit 4 to the previous part.
- Add this 4 to 67 resulting in 71. Keep 1 in this part and carry 7 to the previous part.
- 72 + 7 = 79. Hence, the third digit, from the right, will be 9 and 7 is carried forward.
- 37 + 7 = 44. Keeping 4 of the units place as the fourth digit, carry 4 of the tens place forward to the first part.
- Adding this 4 to the 12 in the first part will result in 16 as the sum. Hence the solution of balancing is 164910.

Addition methods:

a) **By '*Vilokanam*' or observation method**: As addition is a basic mathematical operation, the student is encouraged to 'observe' the numbers to be added and calculate mentally. This method is used to add any number to any other number i.e. there are 2 rows (2 numbers) of addition with multiple columns (multiple digits). Before the method is explained some concepts have to be understood:

- **The end number concept**: When adding two digits, if the sum is a 2 digit number then the last, unit place digit is called the 'end number'. For e.g. 1 + 9 = 10 = 0 is the end number of 10 and 4 + 9 = 13 or 3(end number). Using this concept speeds up the addition process as one calls out only the end number while adding. The end number is to be used from the second set of digits to the last set. The first set of digits is written as the full solution. A table of end numbers is given below and is very important for the student to practice.

Adding	End no.	Adding	End no.
0 + 9 =	9	0 + 8 =	8
1 + 9 =	0	1 + 8 =	9
2 + 9 =	1	2 + 8 =	0
3 + 9 =	2	3 + 8 =	1
4 + 9 =	3	4 + 8 =	2
5 + 9 =	4	5 + 8 =	3
6 + 9 =	5	6 + 8 =	4
7 + 9 =	6	7 + 8 =	5
8 + 9 =	7	8 + 8 =	6
9 + 9 =	8	9 + 8 =	7

Practice Exercise: Complete the above table with numbers from 7 to 1.

- **Carrying & Non-Carrying Numbers concept**: when the sum of two digits is equal to or greater than 10, the digits to be added are called ' carrying numbers' else they are non-carrying numbers'. For e.g. In 8 + 3 = 11, as 11 > 10, 8 and 3 are called carrying numbers and in 4 +2 =6, as 6<10, therefore, 4 and 2 are non-carrying numbers. This concept is important when adding multiple digit numbers together.

Examples : (a) 3672 (b) 5463

$$\begin{array}{r} 3672 \\ +\,5799 \\ \hline 9471 \end{array} \qquad \begin{array}{r} 5463 \\ +\,2426 \\ \hline 7889 \end{array}$$

In (a), starting from the left we add 3 + 5 = 8. This, however, may not be the true sum as the next set of digits (6 + 7 =13) are carrying numbers. Therefore, 8 will be increased by 1 to 9. The second set of digits 6 + 7 = 3(end number) and in this case, as well, the next set of digits are carrying numbers, so 3 will be increased by 1 to 4. Similarly, 7 + 9 = 6 + 1 = 7 and the last set 2 + 9 = 1. So the sum is 9471.

In (b), the first set of digits add up to 7 and since the sum of the next set of digits is 8 which is <10 so, non-carrying numbers. Hence, there will be no change to the sum as no carrying is done, the first digit of the sum will be 7 only. Similarly, since all digit pairs are non-carrying numbers, the result will not be altered and the sum will be 7889.

-The 9's combination exception: While observing the consecutive digit pair sums, we may come across a digit pair sum of 9 i.e. 0+ 9,1 + 8, 2 + 7, 3 + 6, 4 + 5, 5 + 4, 6 + 3, 7 + 2, 8 + 1 or 9 + 0, we cannot immediately identify them as carrying or non-carrying. The solution lies in further observation of the next pair of digits, if the pair is a carrying one, the 9's combination will become a carrying pair or else a non-carrying pair and its sum will be either 0 or 9 respectively.

Examples:	(a) 8654	(b) 5642	(c) 7863
	+ 2382	+ 4358	+1126
	11036	10000	8989

For the examples above, in (a), the 9's combination is followed by carrying numbers. So the pair will be carrying numbers as well and the sum of the previous pair of digit will increase by 1 and the sum of the 9's pair will be 0. In (b), the first 3 digit pairs are 9's combination followed by the last pair, a carrying pair will make the second and third pair carrying numbers as well an the first digit pair will be

10 and the other two will be 0. In (c), there are no carrying pairs, so, the 9' combination remains the same i.e. 9. An important point to remember here is that if the 9's combination appears in the last digit pair, there will be no problem and will be treated as a non-carrying pair.

Practice exercises: Solve a) 26 + 7, b) 89 + 6, c) 55 + 23, d) 125 + 48, e) 345 + 789, f) 1234 + 8765, g) 2456 + 7548, h) 4872 + 6199, i) 7764 + 8238, j) 25673 + 24826.

b) **By the 'dot' method (*Sudha Vidhi*) :** To understand this method, we have to be thorough with the **'end number' concept**. This concept says that when adding two numbers (starting from the units place), if we get a sum ≥ 10,then drop the tens place digit i.e. 1 as a 'dot' next to the second number and take only the end number which is a single digit number. Continue adding all numbers in this way by dropping each 10 as a dot. Once all the numbers are added, count the number of dots. This number is to be carried to the next set of digits on the left. The same method of addition is carried out again. This method is useful when adding multiple numbers with multiple digits.

Example: Add:

```
   1 2 3 4
   5 4 2 3
   4.6.7.9.
 + 8.7.9.2
 ---------
 2 0 1 2 8
```

In the addition above, starting from the top, in the units place start adding the numbers 4 + 3 = 7, 7 + 9 = 6 (from the 16 drop the ten as a dot next to 9) and 6 + 2 = 8. Write 8 in the units place. We can see that there is only 1 dot in the units addition, so we carry 1 to the tens place addition. Adding the tens place digits from the top, we have 1(carried over number) + 3 = 4, 4

+ 2 = 6, 6 + 7 = 3 (dropping the 10 as a dot next to 7) and 3 + 9 = 2 with a dot next to 9. Since there are 2 dots in this addition, we carry over 2 to the 100's place and write 2 in the tens place. Adding the 100s place digits, 2 (carried over) + 2 = 4, 4 + 4 = 8, 8 + 6 = 4 (dot next to 6) and 4 + 7 = 1 (dot next to 7) the 100s place number will be 1 and 2 will be carried to the 1000s place. Next, 2 + 1 = 3, 3 + 5 = 8, 8 + 4 = 2 (dot next to 4) and 2 + 8 = 0 (dot next to 8). After carrying over 2, the sum will be 20128.

With regular practice, this method will become very quick and easy. It is important for the student to read 1 + 9 as 0, 2 + 9 as 1 and 4 + 8 as 2 etc. as they are the end numbers of 10, 11and 12 respectively.

Practice Exercises:

a)	b)	c)
2345	1876	4563
4634	6789	1278
4434	1378	3490
+ 7869	+ 4534	+ 8967

d)	e)	f)	g)	h)
1562	3547	375648	12348	876898
7654	2316	765483	34562	765672
6598	4792	+ 443478	+ 33245	+ 887534
+ 4477	+ 8779			

i)	j)
532146	1567489856
986543	2468642341
+ 213243	+3423564319

Chapter 2.

VYAVAKALANAM / SUBTRACTION

To subtract is to take a part away from a whole. Subtracting a number, often called the '**subtrahend**' from another number, referred to as the '**minuend**', gives us a value called the **difference** of the numbers. This operation is carried out in Vedic mathematics :

a) By the '*Vilokanam*' or observation method: This method is used to subtract two numbers having multiple digits mentally. Before this a few concepts to understand are:

- **The Complement number**: The complement of a number is that when added to the number forms the nearest base number. A base number is usually 10 or a multiple of 10, for e.g. 10, 10^2, 10^3……10^n. The complement of say, 9 is 1 as 9 + 1 =10. Given below is a table to clarify the concept.

Number	Complement	Base	Number	Complement	Base
9	1	10	99	01	100
8	2	10	98	02	100
7	3	10	97	03	100
6	4	10	96	04	100
5	5	10	95	05	100
4	6	10	94	06	100
3	7	10	93	07	100
2	8	10	92	08	100
1	9	10	91	09	100

To find the complement of larger numbers with higher bases, we use the ***Nikhilam*** sutra (all from 9 and last from 10). For e.g. the complement of say, 864538 will be 135462. All the digits from 8 to the penultimate digit 3 is subtracted from 9 to give 13546 and the last digit is subtracted from 10 to give 2.

Practice exercise: Find all complements from 11 to 999.

- **Matched and Mismatched numbers**: When the minuend digit is greater than the subtrahend digit, the digit pair is called a 'matched' pair and subtraction is possible. If the minuend digit is smaller than the subtrahend digit, then the digit pair is a 'mismatched' pair and subtraction is not possible as the difference obtained will be negative. For instance, 7 – 4 is possible as 7>4, hence 7 and 4 are matched numbers but 4 – 7 is not possible as the difference will be -3 as 4<7 so 4 and 7, here, are mismatched numbers.

While subtracting, starting from left to right, we take the pair of digits consecutively and observe if the next pair of digits are matched or mismatched. If matched, there will be no changes needed for the current pair of digit or else the difference of the digits is further reduced by 1 as the mismatched pair will need to borrow 1 from the previous pair to yield a positive answer. For the next pair of digits (if mismatched) we take the complement of the subtrahend and add to the minuend. But before putting this sum down we need to observe the next pair of digits and move forward in a similar manner.

Examples: Solve:

a)	b)
7635	7245
- 5872	- 4133
1763	3112

In (a), the first digit pair is 7 – 5 = 2, but the next digit pair 6 – 8 is a mismatched pair, so the first digit of the difference will be 2 – 1 = 1. The second digit pair is then calculated as 6 + 2(complement of 8) = 8, but the third pair 3 – 7 is mismatched again so the second digit answer will be 8 – 1 =7. The third digit will be 3 + 3(complement of 7) = 6 and since the last pair 5 -2 is matched, the third digit will remain as 6 and the last digit will be 5 – 2 = 3. Hence the difference of the two numbers will be 1763.

In (b), all digit pairs are matched pairs so the difference will be 3112 straight away.

Practice Exercises: Solve:

a)	b)	c)	d)	e)
8456	6751	7768	9342	4589
- 4799	- 3819	- 5892	- 8231	- 1792

- **Same digit pair exception**: When any digit pair, except the first and last pair, are identical for e.g. 4 – 4, or 6 – 6 etc. we cannot say if they are matched or not. This will depend on the next pair of digits being matched or mismatched. If matched, the same digit pair will be matched and result in 0, if not, it will be mismatched and result in 9.

Examples:

a)	b)
6895	8985
- 4829	- 2992
2066	5993

In (a), the second digit pair is same, followed by a matched pair so the difference will be 0 for that pair. The third digit pair is however, followed by a mismatched pair hence 9 - 2 = 7 which will be reduced to 6 and the final digit pair = 5 + 1. So, the difference is 2066.

In (b), the same digit number 9 – 9, is followed by a mismatched pair, 8 – 9, so the difference will be 9 instead of 0. Since the same digit pair is mismatched the difference of the first digit pair will reduce by 1 to 5 and the mismatched third pair will be 8 + 1(complement of 9) = 9. Hence, the answer will be 5993.

Practice Exercises: Solve:

(i) 76342 − 46839

(ii) 567349 − 462392

(iii) 81234765 − 61744792

(iv) 678456345238 − 487656745185

(v) 456758976886 − 352758994789

(vi) 9787695743653346 − 3788755733897823

b) By the '*Nikhilam*' method: Subtracting a number from a base or multiple of a base number involves the use of the *Nikhilam* sutra i.e. *all from 9 and last from 10*. The process of subtraction is to group the minuend digits from the right consisting of the same number of digits as the subtrahend. This will give us a left hand side(LHS) and right hand side(RHS) part of the difference. Reduce the number remaining on the LHS by 1(**Ekanyunena purvena**- '*by 1 less than the one before*') and on the RHS, take the complements from 9 for all digits upto the penultimate digit and the last digit from 10(*Nikhilam*).

Examples:

a)	b)	c)	d)	e)
1 | 0000	4 | 000	8 | 0000	3 | 00000	20 | 00
- 4598	- 1 | 350	- 6987	- 1 | 53289	- 87
5402	2 | 650	7 | 3013	1 | 46711	19 | 13

In the examples above, for (a), the number on the LHS = 1, so reducing it by 1 will give us a 0. And the subtrahend 4598 will be 9-4|9-5|9-9|10-8 = 5402. For (b) the LHS = 4-1 = 3 further reduced by 1 = 2 and RHS 350 = 9-3|10-5 = 650. In this case we ignore the 0 of the last digit and take 5 as the last digit to be converted to its complement from 10. When writing down the answer, however, we will write the 0.For (c),, LHS = 8 – 1 =7 and RHS, 6987 = 3013. For (d), LHS = (3 – 1) -1 = 1 and RHS, 53289 = 46711. Lastly, for (e), LHS = 20 – 1=19 and RHS, 87 = 13.

Practice exercises: Solve: a) 4000 – 356 b) 10000 – 7859 c) 12000 – 28 d) 1000 – 46 e) 71000 – 3467 f) 14000 -67 g) 200000 -3489 h) 61000 – 489 i) 100000 – 4350.

c) By the '*Vinculum*' method: As explained in Part I, (refer Vinculum Vidhi), this method is the quickest and most accurate way to subtract two numbers. It can be done in 2 ways:

- By taking all the digits of the subtrahend as vinculum digits and replacing the subtraction sign '-' by '+'. For instance,

$$\begin{array}{r} 7653 \\ \underline{-\,4578} \\ 31\overline{25} \end{array} \;\Rightarrow\; \begin{array}{r} 7653 \\ \underline{+\overline{4578}} \\ 3075. \end{array}$$

In the subtraction above, we replaced the '-' with '+' and made the subtrahend a vinculum number. On adding $7+\bar{4}=3, 6+\bar{5}=1, 5+\bar{7}=\bar{2}, 3+\bar{8}=\bar{5}$. The sum is $31\overline{25}$. On converting, we reduce the digit before the vinculum by 1 and take the complement of the penultimate vinculum digit from 9 and the last one from 10.

- By directly subtracting the numbers and taking the negative answers, if any, as a vinculum digit. After the operation, converting the vinculum digits to positive digits. In the example above if we directly subtract 4578 from 7653 we will get $31\overline{25}$ as the difference as well, and converting will result in 3075.

Practice Exercises: Solve by Vinculum:

a) $\begin{array}{r} 247 \\ \underline{-\ 98} \end{array}$ b) $\begin{array}{r} 583 \\ \underline{-296} \end{array}$

c) $\begin{array}{r} 663 \\ \underline{-487} \end{array}$ d) $\begin{array}{r} 32547 \\ \underline{-17549} \end{array}$

Chapter 3.

SAMGUNAYA /MULTIPLICATION

Multiplication is an operation when a number, the multiplicand, is multiplied by the multiplier to give a product. In other words the multiplicand is added multiple times(the number of the multiplier) by itself. So, simply put it is a series of additions and the sum is nothing but the product. For example when we multiply say, 7(multiplicand) by 2(multiplier), we are adding 7 twice, so 7 + 7 = 14 and 7 x 2 = 14. The 'x' or '*' is the multiplication sign.

This operation can be done in two ways. The first or general method involves multiplying any number with any number while the second method is more specific as it involves certain conditions or rules for multiplying certain numbers.

A. General method:

Vertically and criss-cross method: The ***Urdhva Triyagbhyam*** sutra is used to multiply any number by any number. This method, when practiced well, is a quick way to multiply any two numbers.

Case 1: To multiply a 2 digit number by another 2 digit number:

The multiplication above involves 3 steps:

(i) Vertically: Starting from the leftmost digits multiply 4 x 3 = 12. Put this number on the LHS.

(ii) Crosswise: The next multiplication will be a criss-cross multiplication and addition, (4 x 4) + (7 x 3) = 37. Put this number next to 12 separating it by a vertical bar.

(iii) Vertically: The final step is to multiply the last set of digits 7 x 4 =28. This number is kept to the rightmost partition. Using the balancing rule and keeping a single digit place for the last two parts we get the product as 1598.

Example:

```
          47
         x34
     12 | 37 | 28 = 1598.
     (i) | (ii)| (iii)
```

The multiplication can be denoted thus: let the 2 digits numbers be ab and cd.

```
a  b      a  b      a  b
↓      |    x    |     ↓
c  d      c  d      c  d
```

For multiplying a 2 digit number by a single digit number, you can add a 0 **before** the single digit and continue as above.

Case 2: 3 digit x 3 digit: In this case there will be 5 steps hence there will be 5 parts to the product.

(i) **Vertically :** Multiply the hundreds place digits vertically and place in the first part.

(ii) **Crosswise:** Multiply the hundreds digit of the first number with the tens digit of the second number and the hundreds digit of the second number to the tens digit of the first number crosswise. Add the two products and place the sum in the second part.

(iii) **Crosswise and vertically:** There will be 3 products. Multiply the hundreds place digit of the first number with the units place digit of the second number, the hundreds place digit of the second number with the units digit of the first number, crosswise, and the tens place digits of both the numbers, vertically. Add all three products and pace this sum in the third part.

(iv) **Crosswise:** Multiply the tens digit of the first number with the units digit of the second number and the tens digit of the second number with the units digit of the first number, crosswise. Add both products and the sum will be the fourth part.

(v)**Vertically:** Finally, multiply both the units digits vertically to get the fifth part of the product.

Apply the balancing technique to give the final product.

An example: Solving:

345 x 289 = 3 x 2 | (3 x 8)+(2 x 4) | (3 x 9)+(2 x 5)+(4 x 8) |
Steps = (i) (ii) (iii)

(4 x 9)+(5 x 8) | 5 x 9 = 6 | 32 | 69 | 76 | 45 = 99705
(iv) (v)

For 3digit * 3digit:

```
a b c   a b c   a b c   a b c   a b c
↓       | x     | X |     x |       ↓
d e f   d e f   d e f   d e f   d e f
```

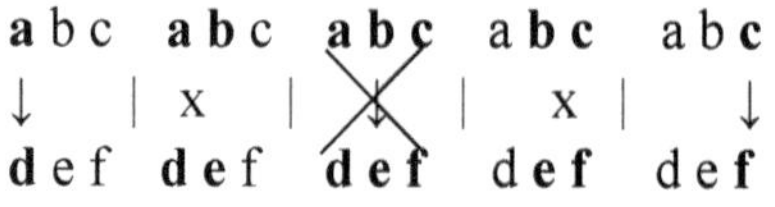

For 4digit * 4digit:

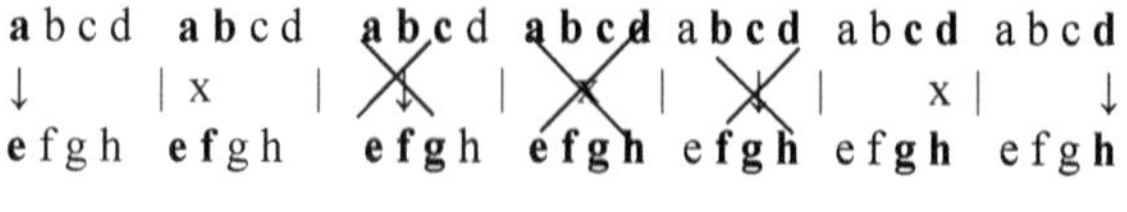

```
a b c d   a b c d   a b c d   a b c d   a b c d   a b c d   a b c d
↓         | x     |   X   |   X   |   X   |     x |         ↓
e f g h   e f g h   e f g h   e f g h   e f g h   e f g h   e f g h
```

This type of multiplication can be carried out with any two numbers. The point to remember is for every digit increase in the numbers the number of steps can be determined by multiplying the number of digits with 2 and subtracting 1 from the product. Case in example, 4 digit x 4 digit will have (4 x 2) -1 = 7 steps.

Practice Exercise: Multiply: (i) 34 x 7 (ii) 48 x 23 (iii) 78 x 89 (iv) 126 x 245 (v) 376 x 298(vi) 678 x 887 (vii) 2348 x 1467 (viii) 4798 x 5688 (ix) 9865 x 8767 (x) 25435 x 32435.

Case 3: For multiplying a large number with a 2digit multiplier, the process is changed a little with the use of **the moving multiplier method**. For example to multiply say, 38451 by 32 we will take the multiplier and its first position will be at the leftmost digits i.e. 38. One important point for this process is that only the first and last digit of the multiplicand will be multiplied vertically. The multiplication of middle digits will be done crosswise only. Solving the example above:

38451	3**84**51	38**45**1	384**51**
32	32	32	32

3 x 3 | (3 x 2)+(3 x 8) | (8 x 2)+(3 x 4) | (4 x 2)+(3 x 5) | (5 x 2)+(3 x 1) | 1 x 2

(i) (ii) (iii) (iv)

= 9 | 30 | 28 | 23 | 13 | 2 = 1230432

The process above involves 4 positions of the multiplier and 4 steps.

i) Position of multiplier is at first two digits of the number. The first digit of the number is multiplied, vertically with the first digit of the multiplier. Then the first digit of number and second digit of the multiplier and second digit of number with first multiplier digit are cross multiplied and added. In the example above = 9 | 30.

ii) The multiplier will then move by 1 digit to the right. Here, under 84. The numbers are cross-multiplied and added giving | 28 | .

iii) Moving to the next digit to the right, the numbers 45 and 32 are cross multiplied and added to result in | 23 |.

iv) Moving right again, the multiplier has reached the last 2 digits, 51 of the number. 51 and 32 are cross multiplied and added. Then the last digit of the number is vertically multiplied with the last digit of the multiplier. The sum and product in this case is | 13 | 2. The result is balanced to give the final product 1230432.

Practice Exercises: Solve : (i) 4644 x 67 (ii) 2387 x 56 (iii) 2145 x 23 (iv) 3471 x 54

B. Specific methods:

1. Base method: The base method of multiplication is derived from the ***Yaavadunam*** sutra meaning 'by the deficiency'. This method of multiplications are done with numbers close to a base. As studied before, the base number is either 10 or a power of 10, i.e. 10^2, 10^3...10^n. There are three conditions that apply here:

a) **Numbers below the base:**

- **For single digit numbers below the base '10'**. The first step is to write down the numbers, one below the other to the LHS. On the RHS, write down the deficiency of each number next to it. The deficiency in this case, is the difference between the base and the number. Since it is deficient, we put a '-' sign before the difference. The next step is to multiply the deficiencies and the product will give us the RHS part of the answer. On the LHS, we take either number and add the negative deficiency of the number.

For e.g. To solve 7 x 9, we take base as 10, deficiency of 7 = 10 – 7 = -3 and deficiency of 9 = 10 – 9 = -1.

7	-3
9	-1

LHS (7+(-1) or (9+(-3) | (-3 x -1)RHS = 6 | 3 = 63.
Hence, 7 x 9 = 63.

- **For 2digit numbers below 100**, the deficiencies are calculated using ***Nikhilam***. Like before, the numbers are placed on the LHS and the deficiencies(d) to the RHS. The multiplication of the deficiencies are the RHS of the product. One point to remember here is that the **number of digit places on the RHS will be equal to the number of 0s in the base**. Here, there will be 2 digit places on the RHS. In case the product is a single digit, add a 0 before the answer, if more than 2 digits, carry the excess to the LHS.

Example:
(i) 98 x 96. Base = 100, d_1 = -2 and d_2 = -4.

98		-2
96		-4
(98 – 4)	|	8 = 94 | 08 = 9408.

(ii) 92 x 94. Base = 100, d_1 = -8 and d_2 = 6, done mentally will result in

86 | 48 = 8648.

(iii) 87 x 77. Base = 100, d_1 = 13 and d_2 =23

87		-13
77		-23
64	|	299 = 6699 (The 2 from the RHS is carried over).

Very large numbers just below the base can be multiplied in two simple steps. For e.g.
76588 x 99998. Base(B) = 100000, d_1 = -23412 and d_2 = - 2.

76588		-23412
99998		- 2
76586	|	46824 = 7658646824.

b) **Numbers above the base:**

This multiplication involves two numbers that are very close to and above their base. The process is identical except that the deficiency or rather the excess is a positive number.

Examples: (i) 107 x 106. B = 100, d_1 = + 7 and d_2 = + 6

107	+ 7	
106	+ 6	
113 |	42	= 11342.

(ii) 1011 x 1004. B = 1000, d_1 = + 11 and d_2 = + 4

1011	+11	
1004	+ 4	
1015 |	044	= 1015044.

c) **One number above and the other below the base:**

In this case, the method will vary a little as we will be dealing with a vinculum number as the deficiencies will be positive and negative and such a product is always negative. To correct this, we have to convert the vinculum to a normal positive number.

Examples: (i) 104 x 97. B = 100, d_1 = +4 and d_2 = -3

$$\begin{array}{ll} 104 & +4 \\ \underline{97} & \underline{-3} \\ 101 \ | & \overline{12} \end{array}$$

= 10088 (see converting Vinculum).

(ii) 1004 x 993. B = 1000, d_1 = +4, d_2 = -7.

$$\begin{array}{ll} 1004 & +4 \\ \underline{993} & \underline{-7} \\ 997 \ | & \overline{028} \end{array} = 996972.$$

If the number of digits of the vinculum is greater than the number of 0s in the base, then we carry over the extra negative digit to the LHS and deduct the same before converting the vinculum.

d) **Numbers with different bases:**

When multiplying two numbers close to a base, one number might be close to one base and the other to another. For e.g. In 9989 x 96, the first number is closer to 10000 and the other to 100. Here, we divide the bases and see that the difference is of a base of 100. Multiplying the said numbers can be shown as below:

$$\begin{array}{rr} 9989 & -11 \\ \underline{\text{x } 96} & \underline{-4} \\ \text{[9(9-4)89] or (9600 -11)} \ | & 44 \end{array} = 958944.$$

The second smaller number is placed with its units digit under the hundreds digit and then its deficiency is multiplied by 100 (the difference) and deducted from the larger number. So, 9989 – (4 x100) = 9589. Alternatively, the smaller number is multiplied by the difference (100 here) to get 9600 and deduct the deficiency of the larger number = 9600 – 11=9589. The deficiencies are multiplied as usual and the digits place of the RHS is equal to the 0s in the lower base.

Practice Exercises: Solve: (i) 97 x 96 (ii) 112 x 108 (iii) 997 x 988 (iv) 986 x 1019(v) 9996 x 9994 (vi) 9993 x 10008 (vii) 99995 x 99981 (viii) 99978 x 100014 (ix) 997 x 98
(x) 1009 x 96.

2. Sub-base method: Sub-bases (SB) are multiples of True Bases (TB). True bases are 10,100, 1000…, while say, 300, 700, 2000, 70000 etc are multiples of 100, 1000, 10000 etc.. Multiplication of numbers that are close to a sub-base follows the same method as above, albeit, with an additional step. The LHS number resulting from the method is increased or decreased, proportionately (***Anurupyena***) while the RHS product of the deficiencies remains the same. Also, the deficiency is calculated from the sub-base.

Examples: (i) For 47 x 42. TB = 10, SB = 5 x 10 = 50, d_1 = 50-47 = -3, d_2 = 50-42 = -8.
(numbers below sub-base)

$$\begin{array}{ll} 47 & -3 \\ \underline{42} & \underline{-8} \\ 5(47-8) \mid 24 & = 5 \times 39 \mid 24 = 195 \mid 24 = 1974 \end{array}$$

(single digit place in RHS)

The LHS sum is increased by multiplying by 5 which is the multiple of base 10. The extra digit on the RHS is carried over.

(ii) 403 x 408. TB = 100, SB = 400, d_1 = +3 and d_2 = +8. (numbers above sub-base)

Multiplying mentally, LHS= 4 x(403 + 8) | 3 x 8 = 161124.

(iii) 512 x 498. TB = 100, SB = 500, d_1 = +12 and d_2= -2. (1 above and other below)

$$\begin{array}{ll} 512 & +12 \\ \underline{498} & \underline{-2} \\ 5(510) \mid & \overline{24} = 2550 \mid \overline{24} = 254976. \end{array}$$

Practice Exercises: Solve: (i)57 x 59 (ii) 79 x 82 (iii) 214 x 226 (iv) 385 x 411 (v) 4112 x 4009 (vi) 7012 x 6989 (vii) 60022 x 60013 (viii) 300012 x 299996.

3. Doubling method: 'Doubling' a number means to multiply the number by 2 or simply to add the same number to it again. For example, 2 x a = 2a or a + a. Before we start doubling a number, let us group the single digits from 0 to 4 as the non-carrying group and 5 to 9 as the carrying group. The table, below, will clarify the concept:

Non-carrying	Carrying
0 + 0 = 0	5 + 5 = 10
1 + 1 = 2	6 + 6 = 12
2 + 2 = 4	7 + 7 = 14
3 + 3 = 6	8 + 8 = 16
4 + 4 = 8	9 + 9 = 18

The reason is that on doubling, 0 to 4 will result in a single digit hence a non-carrying number while 5 to 9, on doubling, will give a sum that has 2 digits (tens place digit is always 1), hence a carrying number. This will help in faster addition. So,

5634 x 2 = 5634 + 5634 = 11268.

Multiplying a number by 4 will entail doubling the number twice and **by 8** will be the result of doubling the number thrice. So,

114 x 4 = 228 x 2 = 456 and 123 x 8 = 246 x 4 = 492 x 2 = 984.

This method is **used to divide any number by 5, 25, 50** . The logic, here, is that the number 5 has a great relationship with 2 as 5 x 2 =10 (a base number). To divide by 5, we can also write 5 as 5 = 10/2. On dividing, this fraction gets inverted and the division becomes a multiplication i.e. Number ÷5 = Number ÷ 10/2 = Number x 2/10. In the same manner 4 x 25 = 100. So any number to be divided by 25 will be multiplied by 4 and divided by 100. The same goes for dividing a number by 50 = 100/2. Multiply the number by 2 and divide by 100.

So on dividing by 5 we double the number and divide by 10 or place a decimal point between the tens and units place.

Example: (i) 445 ÷ 5 = 2 x 445 = 890 ÷ 10 = 89.
(ii) 2345 ÷ 25 = (2345 x 4) ÷100 = 93.80
(iii) 45675 ÷ 50 = (45675 x 2) ÷ 100 = 913.50

Practice Exercises: Solve: (i) 5436 x 2 (ii) 783492 x 2 (iii) 134 x 4 (iv) 6123 x 8
(v) 2347 ÷ 5 (vi) 5647 ÷ 25 (vii) 5678 x 5 (viii) 34987 ÷ 25 (ix) 3478 ÷ 50.

4. Halving method: 'Halving' a number means dividing it by 2. This method is **used to multiply any number by 5, 25, 50** .

To multiply a number by 5, first multiply it by 10 and then divide it by 2, as 10/2 = 5. To multiply a number by 25, multiply first with 100 and divide by 4 (halve the number twice) and so on.

Example: (i) 445 x 5 = 4450÷2= 2225
(ii) 445 x 25 = 44500÷4 = 11125

Practice Exercises: Solve: (i) 45698 x 5 (ii) 67453 x 25 (iii) 5649 x 50 (iv) 38791 x 25.

5. Multiplying with 1's series:

(a) **Multiplying a number with 11, 111, 1111**… involves a series of additions and is a quick and easy method of multiplying large numbers. Points to remember for this process are:

i) The units number of the product is always the same as the units number of the multiplicand.

ii) The number of digits in the product is, at the very least, the total number of digits of both the multiplicand and multiplier less 1.

There are two methods used. The first involves a slightly longer method while the other involves mental calculations.

(i) **Adding 0s method**: Count the multiplier digits and reduce the sum by 1. Take this number of 0s and place on either side of the multiplicand. Then starting from the leftmost 0 of the multiplicand, we group the same number of digits as the multiplier, and put the sum in different partitions. This addition is continued to the last digit (in this case 0) of the number. Then balancing the addition from right to left and keeping one digit place for each part we carry over the extra digits to the next left part. This give us the final product.

Example: Solve 34 x 11.

As the multiplier has two digits add (2 – 1) = 1 zero on both sides of the multiplicand also addition is to be done with 2 digits at a time only. So,
34 x 11 = 0340 = 0 + 3 | 3 + 4 | 3 + 0 = 373.

(ii) **The repeated addition method:** is used to do away with the 0s on either side of the multiplicand making it a quicker process.

Example: 3456 x 111

In the example above, the number of digits of the multiplier is 3. So addition will be done of 3 digits at a time. Since we are not adding 0s the starting digit number is not a 0. Hence, starting from the left write down the first number of the multiplicand. This gives the first number of the product, then add the first digit number and second digit number. This sum is the set in a separate part (in case of carry over). Then add the first, second and third digit and put the sum down in another partition to the right. This completes the first addition of 3 digits and thus the use of the first digit is over. From the second digit, add the second, third and fourth digits. Put this sum in a partition to the right again. This completes the work of the second digit. Moving to the third digit, add the third and last digit and record the sum to the right of the other sums. Since there are no more digits left, the use of the third digit is done. Now finally put the fourth and last digit as it is in the final partition. Now using the balancing method, solve from right to left keeping one digit place in each partition. This will give us the product. So,

3456 x 111 = 3 | 3+4 | 3+4+5 | 4+5+6 | 5+6 | 6 = 383616

Practice Exercises: Solve: (i) 34 x 11 (ii) 87 x 11 (iii) 124 x 111 (iv) 98 x 111 (v) 856 x 111 (vi) 2435 x 1111 (vii) 789 x 1111 (viii) 8878 x 1111.

b) **Multiplying with 12, 13, 14, …….., 19.**

In this method, since the ‘1’ is in tens place, add a ‘0’ to the left of the multiplicand. Then, starting from the right, multiply each digit of the multiplicand by the units digit of the multiplier and add the number to the right of the digit to the product.

Example: 2465 x 12 ≈ 02465
x 12

(2 x 0)+2 | (2 x 2)+4 | (2 x 4)+6 | (2 x 6)+5 | (2 x 5)+0
= 2|8|14|17|10= 29580.

The sutra used here is the ***Sopantya Dvayantam*** or ‘by the ultimate and twice the penultimate’.(refer the sutra) and solved proportionately.

Practice Exercise: Solve: (i) 3245 x 14 (ii) 4523 x 17 (iii) 66789 x 13 (iv) 678432 x 12.

c) **Multiplying with 21, 31, 41, …….., 91.**

In this method the process is reversed. The '0' is placed after the multiplicand. The tens place number is multiplied by the rightmost number(0) and the product is added to the digit on the left.

Example: Solve 2345 x 31 → 23450

$$\begin{array}{r} 23450 \\ \underline{\times 31} \\ 72695 \end{array}$$

In the above example, we add a 0 to the end of 2345. Then multiplying 3(tens place number) with 0 (rightmost number) and adding 5 (number to the left of 0, we get the units number of the product as 5. Multiplying 5 with 3 and adding 4 we get 19 as the product. We put the 9 down in the tens place and carry 1 over to the next multiplication. For the hundreds place of the final product, multiply 4 with 3 and add 3 and 1(carried over) to get 16, place 6 in the hundreds place and carry 1. The thousands place product is (3 x 3) + 2 + 1= 12. Placing 2 here and carrying 1 over, the final product is 3 x 2 = 6 + 1 = 7. Thus the answer is 72695.

Practice Exercise: Solve: (i) 6758 x 41 (ii) 15647 x 61 (iii) 98453 x 21 (iv) 457892 x 81.

6. Multiplying with 9, 99, 999…. : Multiplying a number by 9, 99, 999, 9999…. is a very easy method as long as we remember some rules. The number of digits in the final product will have, at the least, the same number of total digits of the multiplicand and the multiplier. We will now take 3 cases into consideration.

Case 1: Multiplicand digits < multiplier digits.

When multiplying say, 476 x 9999, multiplicand digits (3) are less than multiplier digits (4). We add a 0 **before** the multiplicand to get equal number of digits and then do the operation. The first step is to reduce the multiplicand number by 1 (***Ekanyunam***) and keep this difference as the LHS of the product. For the RHS, starting from the left most digit of the LHS, we take its complement from 9 till the last digit. So,

476 x 9999 = 0476 x 9999 = 0475 | 9524 = 4759524.

Case 2: Multiplicand digits = multiplier digits.

As the digits are equal we can multiply straight away.

276543 x 999999 = 276542 | 723457 = 276542723457.

Case 3: Multiplicand digits > multiplier digits.

Here the multiplication method is different. We first group the number into 2 parts with the second part having the same number of digits as the multiplier. Then, the number in the first part is increased by 1 (***Ekadhikena***). This sum is subtracted from the full multiplicand to give the LHS of the product and for the RHS, from the second part, take complements of all digits from 9 and only the last digit, from 10 (***Nikhilam***). This is the RHS of the product. So, for
763542 x 9999.

We group 763542 as 76 | 3542. Add 1 to 76 = 77. Subtract 763542 – 77 = 763465.
Then, 763542 x 9999 = 763465 | 3542 = 763465 | 6458.
Therefore, 763542 x 9999 = 7634656458.

Practice Exercises: Solve: (i) 67 x 99 (ii) 236 x 999 (iii) 786 x 999 (iv) 2356 x 9999
(v) 984 x 9999 (vi) 10234 x 999 (vii) 2346 x 999 (viii) 23452 x 99999.

7. Multiplying with *Antyayordasakepi*: The upasutra mentioned here translates into '*last totalling 10*'. When multiplying two numbers, if the sum of the units digits = 10 and the other digits are identical, we use this method. The first step is to multiply the units digits and put down the product to the RHS. For the LHS take the number without the units digit and multiply it by one more than the number (***Ekadhikena***). This product will give the LHS of the answer. Balance both sides, keeping 2 digit place in the RHS, to get the final product.

Example: 77 x 73. Units digits sum = 7 + 3 =10 and the tens digits are same i.e. 7. So,
77 x 73 = (7 x (7 + 1)) | 7 x 3 = 5621.

Practice exercises: Solve: (i) 91 x 99 (ii) 72 x 78 (iii) 47 x 43 (iv) 62 x 68 (v) 84 x 86.

There is **one more type** of multiplication, **where the units digits are same and the rest of the number add up to a base number** . In this case, we multiply the units digits and place to the RHS and multiply the rest of the numbers and add the unit digit number to the product. This sum gives the answer on the LHS. If the numbers add up to 100, 1000…, then to the product, add the units number x 10, 100…. to get the correct solution.

Examples :

(i) 27 x 87. Since , 2+8 = 10 (base) and units digit = 7, 27 x 87 = (2 x 8) + 7 | 7 x7 = 2349.

(ii) 42 x 62 = (4 x 6) + 2 | 2 x 2 = 26 | 04 (2 digit place in the RHS). = 2604.

(iii) In 212 x 792, 21 + 79 = 100. So, LHS of product = (21 x 79) + (2 x 10) = 1659 + 20
= 1679 and RHS = 2 x 2 = 04. Then, the product is 167904.

Practice Exercises: Solve: (i) 23 x 83 (ii) 76 x 36 (iii) 376 x 636 (iv) 238 x 778.

8. Factoring method: To simplify the operation using large multipliers, we can take smaller factors of the multiplier and multiply with each factor separately.

To solve 3679 x 24, we consider the factors of 24 = 2 x 12 Then, we double 3679 = 7358 and multiply with 12 = 85056. So **3679 x 24 = 85056**.

Practice Exercises: Solve : (i) 2376 x 33 (ii) 5678 x 26 (iii) 9989 x 30 (iv) 57869 x 36.

9. Repeating numbers: When a number is multiplied by 101, 1001, 10101..... the product seems as if the number is repeating itself.

For example: (i) 78 x 101 = 7878. By Vilokanam, we can feel that the number is being repeatedly multiplied by 01.

(ii) 123 x 101 = 12423. Here the end digit overlaps the first digit, so they have to be added. 123 |123 there are only 2 digit places on the RHS so 1 has to be carried over.

(iii) 678 x 1001 = 678678

(iv) 45 x 1001 = 45045. Since the multiplicand has only 2 digits, we can assume 45 to be 045 so the product will be 045045 = 45045.

(v) 89 x 10101 = 898989.

(vi) 12 x 301 =3612. Using ***Anurupyena***, we first increase 12, proportionately, by 3 which is 36 and then 12. The reverse is also true. 12 x 103 =1236.

This method finds an important application in determining the **percentage increase or decrease of a given number**.

Example:

(i) Increase 23 by 4%. A number can be increased by 1%, 2%...... by multiplying by 1.01, 1.02... . So 23 x 1.04 = 23.92

(ii) Reduce 33 by 3%. To reduce by 3%, we take 1 – 0.03 = 0.97. We can write the same as a vinculum. So 0.97 = $1.0\bar{3}$ and 33 x $1.0\bar{3}$ = $33.\overline{99}$ =32.01.

Practice Exercises: Solve: (i) 23 x 101 (ii) 124 x 101 (iii) 29 x 1001 (iv) 145 x 1001
(v) 56 x 10101 (vi) Increase 46 by 3% (vii) Increase 123 by 4% (viii) Decrease 27 by 2%.

10. Using the Average: The ***Vyashtisamashti*** Sutra (*specific and general*) is another easy method of multiplication of numbers by using their average(A). The deficiency(d) of each number will be the same except that the larger number will be +d and the other, -d. The formula = (A + d)(A - d) = $\mathbf{A^2 - d^2}$ [since $(a + b)(a - b) = a^2 - b^2$]. So the product rule is to **take the square of the average and subtract the square of the deficiency**.

Example: In 63 x 67, A = 65 and d = 2 , ∴ 63 x 67 = $65^2 - 2^2$ = 4225 – 4 = 4221.

Practice Exercise: Solve (i) 35 x 39 (ii) 126 x 122 (iii) 27 x 29 (iv) 83 x 89 (v) 92 x 96.

Chapter 4.

KHANDANAM /DIVISION

Division is another mathematical operation used to segregate a large number into smaller equal groups. The large number is called the Dividend. The separation is done by a smaller number called the Divisor. Each group is represented as a digit called the Quotient. Whatever is left over after the division or is extra, is called the Remainder. In layman's terms, there are as many Divisor values as the Quotient with the additional Remainder. It can be defined as:

Dividend = (Divisor x Quotient) + Remainder.

There are various methods of division, other than the straight lengthy division of Modern Mathematics. These may be general without any constrictions and may be used to divide any number by any number using some sutras and upasutras. The other methods are more specific in nature. They have certain conditions to be met with before the operation can be carried out.

A. General methods:

a) ***Arthur Benjamin* method**: This method of division is helpful in dividing any number by any number. The process involves taking the nearest base (B) or sub-base (SB) of the divisor and calculating the deviation or change from the base/ sub-base. So, the deviation 'd' = (base/sub-base number – divisor). Depending on the base/sub-base being greater than or lesser than the divisor, 'd' will be either positive or negative

Then 'd' becomes the common multiplier. The base/sub-base, after ignoring the last digit (always a 0), becomes the new or modified divisor (MD). In the division process, the 'd' and MD are placed to the upper left and below the divisor respectively, to leftmost side. A dividing line is placed to the right of this. Then, all but the last dividend digits for determining the quotient (Q) are written in this part. The final part, placed after another dividing line to the right of the dividend digits, will have the last digit of the dividend and will give us the remainder (R) of the division.

The MD will divide the digits in the Q portion individually. The remainder from this is carried over to the next digit, placed to the bottom left and this number is the next gross dividend. The first Q number is then multiplied with ‘d’ and the product is placed under the gross dividend.. Both are added vertically to give the new, modified dividend. This will be then divided by the MD to result in the second Q number. This method is continued to the last digit of the dividend to give the R.

If the R number is greater than the divisor, we divide it again to determine the extra Q and write down the final smaller remainder while adding the extra Q to the last number in the Q part to get the final Q.

This division gives us the Q and R as separate values. The R can be represented as a decimal value as well. For this, the division process is continued by placing a decimal point after the last Q digit, and to keep dividing the R digit and place as many ‘0’s required after the R to obtain the requisite number of decimal places.

Example: (i) **Division by a 2-digit divisor:** 53264 ÷ 27.

SB = 30, d = 30 -27 = +3.

	+3	(common multiplier)				
	27	5	$_{2}3$	$_{2}2$	$_{1}6$	$_{1}4$
(MD)	30		3	24	45	60 (Q x d)
			26	46	61	74(R)
(MD x Q)		3	24	45	60	R>27 and 27 x 3 =74,
	(Q)	1	8	(15)	**(20)**	0 = R

Extra Q = **+3** = 1973 = Q.

Hence, 53264 is divisible by 27 with a **Q = 1973 and R = 0.**

(ii) **Division by a 3-digit divisor**: 568784 ÷ 123. SB = 120, d = 120 – 123 = -3.

-3								
123	5	6	$_{8}8$	$_{4}7$	$_{5}8$	$_{4}4$	$_{8}0$	$_{2}0$
120			-12	-18	-6	-12	-6	-18
			76	29	52	**32(R)**	74	2
		48	72	24	48	24	72	
		4	6	2	4	·2	6	

The division above can be carried on dividing the R in the usual way and placing a decimal sign after the last Q digit. Hence, **Q = 4624 or 4624·26 and R = 32**. Therefore, we can obtain a decimal answer up to any number of required digits from further division.

Practice Exercise: Solve: (i) 3452 ÷ 34 (ii) 9768 ÷ 87 (iii) 86548 ÷ 136 (iv) 92456 ÷ 798.

b) ***Dhvajank*** **method**: Dhvajank translates as 'Flag Digit'. In this method of division, the divisor units are grouped into 2. The primary part is called the **Mukhyank** or 'main digit' and is the modified divisor(MD). The second part is placed to the upper right side of the MD and is the flag digit(FD), as well as the common multiplier.

The usual method of 3parts are made, with the divisor in the first part written as MD^{FD}. The second part holds part of the dividend digits, to give us the Q and finally the R part which will hold as many of the last dividend digits as there are digits in the FD.

The main difference in this method is how the multiplier is used. In the case of 2 or more FDs in the divisor, the multiplication with the Q digits will be done using ***Urdhva Triyagbhyam*** or vertically and criss-cross method. The first digit of the Q is multiplied vertically, with the first digit of the flag. After obtaining the second Q digit, both digits are multiplied with the first 2 FDs in a criss-cross and the products are added. This sum is deducted from the corresponding dividend to give the new dividend. This goes on for all dividend digits in the second part while moving to the right to accommodate the correct number of digits. The R portion is dealt with differently.

In case we require the answer up to certain decimal places, this method will continue with a decimal point being placed before the first R digit. If not, then the last Q digits corresponding to the FDs are cross multiplied, added and placed under the first R digit from the dividend. This will continue by repeatedly reducing 1 Q digit from the left and cross- multiplying with the same number of FDs on the right till we reach the last digit of the dividend. Then the last Q will be multiplied by the rightmost FD vertically. The R portion is then balanced and subtracted from the dividend digits in the third part to give the final R.

Example : (i) **2-digit Divisor : 13685 ÷ 24**. MD = 2, FD = 4

```
2 4 | 1 3  36 28 | 5   10  20 20
    |      -20 -28 | 0  -8    0 (FD x Q)
    |       16   0 | 5   2   20 (modified dividend)
    |  10 14   0 | 4   0   18 (MD x Q)
(Q)    5  7   0 |· 2   0    9
```

Q =570 or 570·209 and R = 5

(ii) **3-digit Divisor: 3725687 ÷ 407**. MD = 4, FD = 07.

```
4 07 | 3  7  12 85 26  | 38  7 (2 digits in FD)
     |         0  63  7 | 35 28 (balancing rule)
     |        12  22 19 | 378( balanced)
     |   36    4  20 16 | (387 – 378)
          9    1   5  4 |  9
```

Q = 9154 R = 9.

In the division above, we can take 4 as the MD and the FD = 07. So, the R part will have the last 2 digits of the dividend corresponding to the number of digits in the flag. Since 4 cannot divide 3, we take the first 2 dividend digits i.e. 37. This is divided by 4 giving Q = 9 and R = 1. The 1 is carried to the next digit to give a dividend of 12. The Q is multiplied, vertically with 0 (first digit of FD). The product is 0 which when deducted from the dividend gives the new dividend as 12 again. This 12 is divisible by 4 where Q =3 and R = 0. But one thing we have to be careful is that the next dividend will be 5 and the FD x Q = 07 x 93(Q digits) when cross multiplied and added will amount to (7 x 9) + (0 x 3) = 63. Deducting this number will give us a negative new dividend. This cannot be divided so we reduce the second Q to 1 instead of 3. This gives an R = (12

– 4) = 8. So the next dividend will be 85 and the FD x Q = 63. Therefore, the new dividend will be 85 – 63 = 22. This divided by 4 gives Q = 5 and R = 2. The next dividend is 26, FD x Q = 07 x 15 (2 FD with 2 Q digits max.) = (7 x 1) + (0 x 5) = 7. Reducing this number will make the new dividend 19 and is divided by 4 with Q = 4 and R = 3. Since this was the last digit to be divided in the Q part, we have the Q = 9154.

If the answer is required in decimals, the above method of division will be continued with each R part digit. Otherwise, the new dividend = 387 and the FD x Q for the first R digit = 07 x 54 = 35. Placing this under the first R digit, we take the FD x Q = 7 x 4(last digits of Q and FD multiplied vertically) = 28. Place this under the last R digit. Now, balancing 35 | 28 = 378. This number is subtracted from the new dividend to give the final R = 9.

Practice Exercise: Solve: (i) 4525 ÷ 34 (ii) 87634 ÷ 96 (iii) 14536 ÷ 123 (iv) 563725 ÷ 721

B. **Specific methods:**

a) ***Nikhilam*** **method**: The Nikhilam or 'Base' method of division is carried out when the divisor is just under a base. The first step is to group the digits from the right with the same number of digits as the divisor. The method will be operated on these groups. The process is to create three partitions. The first to hold the divisor, the second for the quotient digits and the last group for the remainder digits. The divisor is put down in the first group. The deviation (d) = Base – Divisor is placed under the divisor with a 0 or 0s depending on the divisor digits. Then d becomes the common multiplier.

The division is done by writing down the first group of dividend digits as is. This is the first part of the quotient (Q). This number is then multiplied by d and added to the next set of digits. This sum is the next group of Q. This multiplication with d and consequent addition with the next group of digits is continued till the last set. The sum of the last set is the remainder (R). If the remainder is greater than the divisor we divide this by the divisor and the quotient thus obtained is added to the rest of Q and the leftover part is the final R.

i) **For Base = 10**. As the divisor is under 10 or a single digit only the last digit of the dividend will be placed in the R portion. The rest of the number is kept in Q.

Examples: 1) **31÷8.** B = 10, d = 10 – 8 = 2

8 | 3 | 1

2 | | 6 (3 x 2)

3 | 7. So, **Q = 3 and R = 7**

2) **5329 ÷ 6**; d = 4

6 | 5 3 2 | 9

4 | 20 92 | 376

5 23 94 | 385 . 385 ÷ 6 = 64.

+64 (extra quotient)

8 8 8 = Q & R = 1

ii) **For Base =100**. 2 digits in divisor will entail 2 digits in the remainder portion and the quotient portion also grouped as 2 digits. The d is written with a 0 before it if single.

Examples: 1) **156 ÷ 98**; d = 100 – 98 = 02.

98 | 1 | 56

02 | | 02

| 1 | 58 Hence, **Q = 1 and R = 58.**

2) **2507 ÷ 97**; d = 03.

97 | 25 | 07

03 | | 75

25 | 82. , **Q = 25 and R = 82**

iii) **For Base = 1000**; R = 3 digits, Q = set of 3 digits and d = 3 digits.

Example: **12345 ÷ 994**; d = 006.

994 | 12 | 345

006 | | 072

12 | 417 **Q = 12 and R = 417.**

This division is possible with as big a base as possible. Hence large numbers may be divided by large numbers as long as the divisors are just under a suitable base.

Practice Exercise: Solve: (i) 46 ÷ 7 (ii) 1238 ÷ 94 (iii) 8796 ÷ 87 (iv) 23765 ÷ 993.

b) ***Paravartya* method**: Derived from the sutra '***Paravartya Yojayet***' meaning '*to transpose and apply*', is the method used to divide numbers whose divisors are above a base. There is no calculation of 'd'. The divisor digits are placed under the divisor again by ignoring the first digit(base first digit). The rest of the digits are transposed, i.e. each digit will become a vinculum or negative digit and this is the common multiplier. This process will have 2 parts, the divisor and the dividend. The quotient digits and the remainder digits are calculated after the division. The number of Q digits is the difference of the digits of the dividend and divisor plus 1.

Say, in dividing 1234 by 112, B = 100, Q digits Q(n) = (4 – 3) + 1 = 2. The rest of the digits make up the remainder part.

112	1	2	3	4	
-1 -2		-1	-2		
			-1	-2	
	1	1	0	2	Here, **Q = 11 and R = 2.**

The division is done by first bringing down the first digit of the dividend as is. The next step is to multiply this to the two vinculum numbers individually and place them under the second and third digit respectively. Solve for the second digit and again multiply this result with the vinculum digits and place under the third and fourth digit. This process is repeated till the last digit of the dividend is covered. The answer of the division is then grouped for the Q and R as discussed earlier.

Examples: 1) 456783 ÷123. B = 100 and Q(n) = 4.

1 2 3	4	5	6	7	8	3
-2 -3		-8	-12			
			6	9		
				0	0	
					-32	-48
	4	(-3)	0	(16)	(-24)	(-45)

Q(n) = 4, so, Q = 4$\bar{3}$16 = 3716. Solving for R =$\overline{285}$, we take a multiple of 123 that is greater than 285 that when added to its negative form, will give a positive remainder. In this case, 123 x 3 = 369 which on adding with -285 = 84. This is the true R.

The quotient is reduced by 3 that has been used to convert the vinculum. Therefore, **Q = 3713 and R =84.**

2) 276587 ÷ 13113. B = 10000, Q(n) = 2.

```
13  1 1 3 | 2  7  6  5  8  7
-3 -1 -1 -3 |     -6 -2 -2 -6
                     -3 -1 -1 -3
______________________________
              2  1   1  2  1  4
```

Q = 21 and R = 1214.

Practice Exercise: Solve: (i) 5673 ÷ 112 (ii) 87347 ÷ 124 (iii) 85321 ÷ 1013 (iv) 453789 ÷ 1023 (v) 6543768 ÷ 12132.

c) **Division with the 9s series:**

Dividing a number with 9, 99, 999…etc. is simply a series of additions and can be best explained with an example.

Example: (i) 3221 ÷ 9 → 9 | 3 2 2 | 1

| 3 5 7 | 8 → Q = 357 and R = 8

(ii) 75834123 ÷ 99 → 99 | 75 83 41 | 23

75 (158) (199) | (222).

R = 222> 99, 222/99 →Q = 2 and R = 24. ∴ Q = 75 | 158 | 199 + 2 = 766001.

Hence Q =766001 and R = 24.

In the divisions above, division by a single digit will have 1 digit in the R and 1 digit place in the Q while a 2 digit divisor will entail a 2 digit R and the dividend is grouped into 2 digits.

Hence, in (i) the first digit is brought down as is and for the next Q this is added to the next dividend number. This sum is placed next to the first Q and is then added to the next dividend number.

This method is continued till the last digit of the dividend which is the remainder part. If the value of the remainder is greater than the divisor, it is further divided to give the extra Q and the final R. In (ii), the dividend is grouped as per the digits in the divisor also keeping the last group for the remainder. The first group is brought down as in the previous example, as is and added to the next group and so on.

The resultant R = 222 which is greater than the divisor and on dividing it by 99 again we get the extra Q as 2 with the final R = 24. This extra Q is added to the penultimate group giving 201 as the sum. Keeping the last 2 digits of the sum 01, the extra 2 is carried over and continued thus till the first group. So, 158 + 2 = 160, and 75 + 1 = 76, will result in
Q = 766001 and R =24.

Note: Dividing by 8, 7, 6 can be done in the same way. The difference of each number from 10 is 2,3 and 4 respectively, so when dividing with 8, the Q is multiplied by 2 or doubled and then added to the next dividend number. The Q in each case is increased proportionately increased before the addition process.

Practice Exercise: Solve: (i) 6753 ÷ 9 (ii) 76523 ÷ 99 (iii) 435647 ÷ 999 (iv) 4562 ÷ 8.

d) **Division with 11, 12, 13... :**

While dividing with 9, 8, 7and 6, the divisor was 1, 2, 3 and 4 less than 10 respectively. Here the divisor is 1, 2, 3.. more than 10. So the method involves subtraction of each Q number from the next dividend number, accordingly.

Example: 1341 ÷ 11 → 11 | 1 3 4 | 1

1 2 2 | $\bar{1}$ (1 – 2)

Since, R is negative, we borrow **one** 11 from the Q and add it to the R = 11 + (-1) =10 and reduce the Q by 1 to 121. Therefore, Q = 121 and R = 10.

When dividing by 12, 13 etc. multiply the first Q by 2,3..etc. and then deduct from the next dividend.

Practice Exercise: Solve: (i) 13453 ÷ 11 (ii) 34256 ÷ 12 (iii) 395278 ÷ 13.

Chapter 5.

COMBINED OPERATIONS

Combined operations in arithmetic is a good exercise in practicing left to right calculations, giving us this flexibility along with the choice of using vinculum as and when needed to ease the method and increase speed of calculations in one line.

A. Sum of products:

(i) (43 x 8) + (54 x 3) = [(4 x 8) + (5 x 3)] + [(3 x 8) + (4 x 3)] = $5\bar{3}06$ =506.

To find the first figure of the sum above, we multiply 4 by 8 and 5 by 3 and add the products to get 47. Since the unit digit is a large number and will entail a carrying number, we can take the vinculum of 47 = $5\,\bar{3}$ and put that down. We then multiply 3 by 8 and 4 by 3, the sum of which will be 36. We deduct $\overline{30}$ from the left to get 06 and put it down. Hence the final sum is 506.

(ii) (1237 x 4) + (342 x 7) + (56 x 2) = $4\ {}^{3}\bar{1}\ {}^{5}0\ {}^{5}4$ = 7454.

In the above addition, to find the thousands place sum, multiply 1 by 4 and put this down. For the hundreds place multiply 2 by 4 and 3 by 7. On adding the products we get 29. We put this as a vinculum with the 3 placed to the top left of -1 to be carried over. The tens place
sum = 3 x 4 + 4 x 7 + 5 x 2 = 50. Put down the 0 with 5 to be carried over to its top left. The units place adds up to 54. We place 4 in its place and 5 on the left to be carried over, resulting in 7454(4 +3 | -1 + 5 | 0 +5 | 4).

(iii) (65 x34) + (23 x 32) = $2_4 9_2 46$ = 2946.

Using the vertically and crosswise multiplication method, we multiply 6 x 3 and 2 x 3. Their sum is 24. Put 2 and place 4 to its right bottom. The next crosswise multiplication will be [6 x 4 + 5 x 3] + [2 x 2 + 3 x 3] = 52. Now adding 40 carried over from the left = 92. Pace 9 as the next number in the sum and 2 to its right bottom. The final vertical multiplication is 5 x 4 and 3 x 2 = 26 + 20(from the left) = 46. Put this down and the final sum will be 2946.

B. Sum of Squares:

(i) $43^2 + 54^2 = 4_1 7_4 65 = 4765$.

Here we use the Duplex method. The duplex of the first digits is added to get 41. Put 4 as the first figure of the sum and 1 to its left bottom. Next take the Duplex of both digits and ythe sum is 64. Add 10 from the left to get 74. So, 7 is the next figure and 4 is to be carried over. Finally take the Duplex of the last digits. The sum is 25 and the final figures are 25 + 40 = 65.

(ii) $(13425 \times 34) + 213^2 = 3\,{}^{2}\bar{3}\;{}^{3}\bar{2}\;{}^{3}5\;{}^{3}\bar{1}\;{}^{3}\bar{1} = 501819$.

In this addition, we use both the moving multiplier and Duplex methods. For the first figure we multiply 1 by 3 = 3 followed by five 0s and the Duplex of 2 gives 4 followed by four 0s. So, the latter will come in for the thousands place sum. Hence, we put 3 as the first number. Next, imagine the multiplier 34 placed under 13. The cross multiplication sum = 13. Add the 4 from the Duplex. The sum now is 17. We put this as a vinculum as 2 to be carried over and -3 as the second place number. Moving the 34 under 34, cross multiplying and adding will result in 24. Adding D(21) to this = 28. Converting to vinculum, we keep up the calculations till the last digits vertical multiplication added to the Duplex of last digit of the square. Solving, we get 501819.

The same method may be used for difference of products and for difference of squares.

C. Division of additions:

(i) (86 + 47 + 91 + 38) ÷ 7 = $3_3 7_3$ = Q = 37 R =3.

Adding the tens digits, we get 24 which when divided by 7 gives Q = 3, R = 3. Putting this as the first Q digit with the R to the bottom right. Adding the units digits = 22 + 30 = 52÷7 → Q = 7 R = 3. So, Q =37 and R =3. If the divisor has 2 digits , use the Flag method of division.

(ii) (32 x 8 + 41 x 4) ÷ 9 = $4_4 6_6$ → Q = 46 and R = 6.

Here, multiply the tens digits, add and divide by 9 followed by the units digits in the same manner.

(iii) ($14^2 + 28^2 + 52^2$) ÷ 8 = $3_6\ {}^15_0\ {}^10_4$ = Q =460 and R = 4

Take the relevant Duplexes, add and divide by 8 each time to get the solution.

Practice exercises: Solve: (i) (567 x 8) + (782 x 9) (ii) (28 x 45) + (56 x 32)

(iii) $48^2 + 64^2 + 88^2$ (iv) (35647 x 27) + 325^2 (v) (456 +789 + 623 + 532) ÷ 7

(vi) (62 x 43 + 23 x 13) ÷ 8 (vii) ($87^2 + 37^2 + 66^2$) ÷ 6 (viii) (378 + 552 + 879) ÷ 56.

Chapter 6.

AUSHATA /AVERAGE

'Average' is the name given to a single number to represent a group of numbers. It is also called the 'arithmetic mean'. The formula for calculating the average of a group of numbers is:op

$$\text{Average} = \frac{\text{Sum of all the numbers in the group}}{\text{Total numbers in the group}}$$

Some important observations:

1. To find the average(A) of a group of consecutive numbers or numbers in arithmetic progression (n), then the (n + 1)/2 th number in the sequence is the average. For e.g. 2, 4, **6**, 8. 10 is a set of numbers with a group set n = 5, then the (5 +1)/2 = 3rd number of the set i.e. **6** is the average.

2. If the group set is an even one, then the middle two numbers are added and divided by 2 to get the average. For e.g. 2, 4, **6, 8**, 10, 12 will have its average between 6 and 8 and is calculated as (6 + 8) /2 = **7.**

3. The average of the first 'n' odd numbers is 'n'. For e.g. In 1, **3, 5**, 7, n = 4 and average of the above set is (3 + 5)/2 = **4** = n.

4. The average of the first 'n' even numbers is n+1. For e.g. In the set 2, 4, **6**, 8, 10, where n = 5, the average will be 5 + 1 = **6.**

5. The average of the first ‘n’ natural numbers is (n + 1)/2. For e.g. In the set 1, 2, **3, 4**, 5, 6, n = 6 so average is (6 + 1)/2 = **3.5** = (3 + 4)/2.

6. The average of a set of consecutive numbers is equal to the average of the first and last numbers. For e.g. in the set 12, 13, 14, 15, 16, the average is 14 and the average of the first and last number = (12 + 16)/2 = 14 also.

7. For any set of numbers, if each of the numbers is increased/decreased by another number individually, the average of the set also increases/decreases by that number whether it is by addition, subtraction or multiplication.

   Example: for a set 2, 6, 8, 12, 19, 7 the A = (2 + 6 + 8 + 12 + 19 + 7)/6 = 9.

   Adding 2 to each number we get the set as 4, 8, 10, 14, 21, 9 and A= 66/6 = 11.(9+2)
   Deducting 1 from all, we get 1, 5, 7, 11, 18, 6 and A = 48/6 = 8 (9 -1).
   Multiplying each by 3, we get 6, 18, 24, 36, 57, 21 and A = 162/6 = 27 (9*3).

8. The sum (S) of a set of numbers (n) = Its average (A) * (n). When the average of a set of numbers is given along with the separate averages (say, A_1 and A_2) of the first n / 2 numbers and the last n / 2 numbers, we observe that the middle number(m) is repeated and overlaps. Traditionally, to find the value of ‘m’, we find the sum of the first n /2 and that of the next n / 2 numbers and deduct the sum of n from it i.e.

   m = (A_1 * first n / 2 + A_2 * last n / 2) – A * n.

This is a longer process, instead we use ‘Yaavadunam’ or ‘by the deficiency here. We take the deficiency of A from A_1 and A_2 and multiply each n/2. The sum of the products and A is ‘m’.

Example: The average of 11 numbers is 16. The average of the first 6 numbers is 15 and the last 6 numbers is 19. Find the middle number.

In the example above, the first 6 and the last 6 numbers add up to 12 but we have only 11 numbers. So, it is clear that the middle number is repeated.
The deviation (A1 – A) = -1 and sum of the first 6 numbers = -1*6 = -6.
The deviation (A2 – A) = +3and sum of the last 6 numbers = +3*6 = 18.
So, m = 16 + (-6 +18) = 28. Hence, the middle number is 28.

9. Sometimes, a number (N) from a set (n) is replaced by another number (N_1) and the average (A), either increases or decreases by this process. To find the value of N_1 we need to know the value of N and also the total increase or decrease. As observed above in point 7, if the average increases or decreases by a certain quantity, the rest of the numbers in the set also increase or decrease by the same number. Let the change in A be denoted by ‘c’, then the total change = c * n. This product is added to N to get the value of N_1.

Example: The average age of a group of 12 workers is 28. If one worker, whose age is 25, leaves and another worker replaces him, the average becomes 29. What is the age of the new worker?

Here, c = 29 – 28 = +1 and total change = +1 * 12 = 12 and N = 25.
So, N_1 = 25 + 12 = 37. Therefore, the age of the new worker is 37.

10. When the average (A) is deducted from every number in a set (n), we get its deviation (D) from A. The sum of all 'n' deviations is always equal to zero. This observation is useful to:

a) Find the value of an unknown number in the set.

Example: In the set 3, 5, 8, 12, 17, x, 23, 29, find x if the average is 16.

Taking deviations of each number D = (N – A) we have, (-13) + (-11) + (-8) + (-4) + (+1) + (+7) + (+13) = -15. But sum of all deviations is 0, so we have to add +15 to A to get it. This will also be the value of x.
So, x = 16 + 15 = 31.

b) Find the average (A) of a set (n) of numbers when the averages of sub-groups of the set are given.

Example: There is a group of 15 girls in a classroom. 5 girls weigh 42kgs, 5 other girls weigh 44kgs and the rest weigh 46kgs. What is the average weight of the girls in the classroom.

Here, we take the middle value of the weight 44kgs and compare it with the other two. So, deviation for 42kgs = 42 – 44 = -2 and that of 46kgs = 46 – 44 = +2. Adding them we get a 0. So, 44kgs is the average weight of the 15 girls.

Practice Exercises:

A. Find the average: (i) 52, 54, 56, 58, 60 (ii) 3, 7, 11, 15, 17, 19.

B. Find x: (i) 34, x, 36, 38, 42, 46 if average(A) is 40. (ii) 12, 15, 22, x, 28 if A = 20.

C. Solve:

(i) The average weight of a group of 8 men is 70 kgs. One man weighing 65 kgs leaves and another man is hired in his place. The average weight increases by 1.5 kgs. Find the weight of the new man.

(ii) In a classroom the average age of 12 students and 1 teacher is 20. The average age of 9 students is 15, and the average age of the rest of the students is 16. Find the age of the teacher.

11. In a random set of numbers, the average or mean is, at times not usually the middle value. It means that the set of numbers are spread out unevenly from the mean or average. One way to is to find their mean deviation from the mean or average. This means to find how far each of the numbers are from the average and to find the average of these deviations. This is done by adding the deviations and dividing by the total numbers in the set.
Example: Find the mean deviation of 23, 31, 42, 55, 64. Let the mean of the numbers be $\bar{x} = (23 + 31 + 42 + 55 + 64) \div 5 = 43$. To find the mean deviation we subtract the mean from each number to get:
-20, -12, -1, +12, +21. Adding them, we get '0' as the sum as seen above. So, we can either ignore the '-' signs and add all the numbers and divide by 5 or we take one set positive or negative, add them, double the sum and divide by 5. The **mean deviation** is, therefore, 2(33) ÷ 5 = **13.2.**

Practice Exercise: Find the mean and mean deviation of: (i) 30, 40, 43, 48, 49. (ii) 17, 34, 53, 81, 36, 31 (iii) 5, 7, 8, 12, 13. (iv) 20, 30 ,40, 50, 65.

Chapter 7:

PRATISHATA /PERCENTAGES

'Percent' stands 'for every hundred'. It is the number or ratio represented as a fraction of 100. It is represented as '%'. So, 25% = 25/100 = 0.25 or ¼ in its smallest form, as a decimal, fraction or a part of 100. This number has no dimension nor any measurement unit.

Calculating percentages:

(i) Percentage is used to specify a portion of a whole. So, 25% of a certain quantity 'Q' is calculated as
$\frac{25}{100}$ x Q

Example: What is 45% of 1234? → (45/100) * 1234 = 555.30
.

(ii) If the percentage is a large number the calculation can be done by splitting the number.

Example: 64% of 83 ? → [(60 + 4)/100] * 83 = (4980 + 332)/100 = 53.12.

(iii) When a part of a number is given, we divide both numbers and multiply by 100.

Example: What percent is 945 of 5670? → (945/5670) * 100 = 16.66%

Practice Exercise: (i) What is 24 % of 6240? (ii) What is 78% of 456387?

(iii) What percentage is 560 of 97450? (iv) Calculate the percent of 475 of 7780.

Percentages have a lot of applications. Measuring Simple/ Compound Interest on an amount of money, measuring proportionately in mixing a compound, comparing age, weight, salary, etc.. Any changes made to the whole will cause a proportionate change in the percentage. This change could be either an increase or decrease.

Percentage Increase: A percentage increase in a quantity, when calculated will have the whole and an additional percentage of the whole. So, a 1%, 2%, 3% …. increase will be calculated by multiplying the quantity by 1.01, 1.02, 1.03…

Example: (i) Increase 36 by 2% = 36 x 1.02 = 36.72
(ii) Increase 765 by 4% = 765 x 1.04 = 795.60

Percentage Decrease: A percentage decrease in a quantity involves the deduction of the percent from the whole. So, a 1%, 2%, 3%.... decrease in quantity will be calculated by multiplying the quantity by 0.99, 0.98, 0.97 etc.. To make the calculation simpler we take the vinculum of the multiplier. Hence, the decrease is measured by multiplying the quantity by $1.0\bar{1}$, $1.0\bar{2}$, etc.

Example (i) Decrease 678 by 3% = 678 x $1.0\bar{3}$ = 657.66
(ii) Decrease 9783 by 5% = 9783 x $1.0\bar{5}$ = 9293.85

Practice Exercise: (i) Increase 34 by 10% (ii) Increase 69345 by 7% (iii) Increase 455 by 12% (iv) Decrease 3789 by 6% (v) Decrease 49653 by 4%.

Percentage is relative with no measurement unit. Also, when we increase a quantity by a certain percentage and then decrease this by the same percentage. The final quantity will not be the same as the increase is in the original quantity but the decrease is done on the increased quantity.

For e.g. Increase 500 by 2% = 500 x 1.02 = 510. Then decrease by 2% = 510 x $1.0\bar{2}$ = 499.8.

Example: A earns 20% less than B. By what percent more does B earn than A?

Let B earn Rs. 100, the A earns 20% less i.e. Rs. 80. So, B earns Rs 20 more than A

∴ B earns (20/80) x 100 = 25% more than A.

To convert a percentage to a decimal or fraction will entail dividing the %age by 100.

∴ 45% = 45/100 = 0.45 (decimal) or $\frac{9}{20}$ (fraction).

To convert a decimal or a fraction to a percentage, multiply by 100.

∴ 0.125 x 100 = 12.5% and $\frac{1}{8}$ x 100 = 12.5%.

Chapter 8.

APURNAANKA / FRACTION

A fraction is defined as a part of the whole. When a whole is divided into equal parts, one equal part is called its fraction and is denoted as $\frac{a}{b}$ where 'a', called the Numerator (N), is a part of a whole that has 'b' (called the Denominator(D)) number of equal parts.

A. **Types of fractions:** There are 3 types of fractions:

a) **Proper fraction:** A proper fraction is one where the N<D. for e.g.$\frac{3}{5}, \frac{7}{9}, \frac{5}{8}, \frac{3}{7}$ are all proper fractions.

b) **Improper fraction:** An improper fraction is one that has the N>D. So, $\frac{21}{4}, \frac{23}{8}, \frac{24}{7}$ are examples of improper fractions.

c) **Mixed fraction:** A mixed fraction is an improper fraction divided into a whole number and proper fraction. Thus, $\frac{24}{7} = 3\frac{3}{7}$, is an example of an improper fraction being divided by 7 to give 3 as the whole number and the remainder (24 – 21(7*3)) = 3 and is denoted as a proper fraction with N = 3 and D = 7, and $3\frac{3}{7}$ is called a mixed fraction. It may be written as $3\frac{3}{7}$ or $3 + \frac{3}{7}$. A mixed fraction can be reconverted to an improper fraction by multiplying the whole number by D and adding N. Therefore, $3\frac{3}{7} = \frac{3*7+3}{7} = \frac{24}{7}$.

Practice Exercise: Name the fraction: (i) $\frac{5}{13}$ (ii) $\frac{16}{11}$ (iii) $\frac{151}{13}$ (iv) $\frac{7}{19}$ (v) $\frac{18}{17}$ (vi) $5\frac{3}{11}$

B. Ascending Order & Descending Order: When one is given a number of proper fractions and are asked to put them in ascending (lowest to highest) order or descending (highest to lowest) order we need to compare the fractions 2 at a time. Multiply the N from the first and the D from the second, as well as N of the second with the D of the first in a criss-cross manner. Compare the products and place the higher fraction to the left/right of the lower one. Again compare the lower on to the next and put the lower one to the extreme left/right. Continue in this manner, till all fractions are compared and put in the correct order.

For e.g. put $\frac{3}{5}, \frac{7}{9}, \frac{5}{8}, \frac{3}{7}$ in ascending order. We take the first 2 fractions and multiply their N and D in a criss-cross manner. Therefore, 3*9 < 7*5. We keep the lower fraction to the left of the higher one. Next, comparing the first and third fraction, we have 3*8 <5*5 and comparing the second to the third we have 7*8 >9*5. We can observe that the second fraction is bigger than the third fraction. So, we place the third fraction between the first and second. Comparing the third to the last, we have 5*7>8*3 and the first with the last we have 3*7 >3*5. Hence, we can see that the last fraction is the smallest, followed by the first, third and finally the second. This order is called the ascending order (A.O) moving from the lowest to the highest. To present them in descending order (D.O), we write them in reverse.

$\therefore \frac{3}{5}, \frac{7}{9}, \frac{5}{8}, \frac{3}{7} \rightarrow$ A.O $= \frac{3}{7}, \frac{3}{5}, \frac{5}{8}, \frac{7}{9}$, and D.O $= \frac{7}{9}, \frac{5}{8}, \frac{3}{5}, \frac{3}{7}$,

Practice Exercise: 1. Sort in A.O: (i) $\frac{3}{5}, \frac{4}{9}, \frac{6}{13} \frac{7}{15}$ (ii) $\frac{4}{7}, \frac{5}{8}, \frac{6}{11}, \frac{7}{13}$ (iii) $\frac{2}{5}, \frac{2}{7}, \frac{2}{9}, \frac{2}{3}$.

2. Sort in D.O: (i) $\frac{3}{5}, \frac{2}{7}, \frac{6}{17}, \frac{4}{13}$ (ii) $\frac{5}{8}, \frac{2}{9}, \frac{1}{7}, \frac{6}{13}$ (iii) $\frac{4}{11}, \frac{3}{7}, \frac{5}{9}, \frac{8}{15}, \frac{9}{19}$ (iv) $\frac{11}{13}, \frac{13}{17}, \frac{15}{19}, \frac{17}{19}, \frac{2}{3}$

C. **Operations on fractions:** Mathematical operations like addition, subtraction, multiplication and division, can be performed on all types of fractions.

a) **Addition:** The method to add two fraction say, $\frac{a}{b}$ and $\frac{c}{d}$ is to cross multiply a*d and b*c and add them to get the final N and multiply b*d for the final D. this can be denoted as:

$$\frac{a}{b} + \frac{c}{d} = \frac{ad + bc}{bd}$$

For proper fractions:

Example: Add: $\frac{3}{7} + \frac{6}{11} = \frac{3*11+7*6}{7*11} = \frac{75}{77}$

Practice Exercise: Add: (i) $\frac{4}{9} + \frac{7}{13}$ (ii) $\frac{11}{13} + \frac{3}{7}$ (iii) $\frac{2}{9} + \frac{5}{8}$ (iv) $\frac{8}{13} + \frac{3}{5}$ (v) $\frac{6}{13} + \frac{1}{11}$

For improper fractions:

Example: Add: $\frac{21}{5} + \frac{37}{11} = \frac{21*11+37*5}{5*11} = \frac{416}{55}$.

Practice Exercise: Add: (i) $\frac{14}{9} + \frac{17}{13}$ (ii) $\frac{11}{3} + \frac{23}{7}$ (iii) $\frac{42}{9} + \frac{35}{8}$ (iv) $\frac{38}{13} + \frac{33}{5}$

For mixed fractions: The method here will be a little different. The whole number parts of both numbers are added together and the fraction parts are added separately.

Example: Add: $3\frac{3}{5} + 7\frac{7}{8} = (3 + 7) + (\frac{3*8+7*5}{5*8}) = 10\frac{59}{40} = 11\frac{19}{40}$

Practice Exercise: Add: (i) $5\frac{4}{7} + 2\frac{3}{8}$ (ii) $9\frac{1}{4} + 3\frac{5}{6}$ (iii) $6\frac{4}{7} + 8\frac{2}{9}$

b) **Subtraction:** The subtraction method is similar to the addition method. Instead of adding the cross multiplication products we find the difference between them. It may be represented as:

$$\frac{a}{b} - \frac{c}{d} = \frac{ad - bc}{bd}$$

For proper fractions:

Example: Subtract: $\frac{6}{7} - \frac{5}{11} = \frac{6*11-7*5}{7*11} = \frac{31}{77}$

Practice Exercise: Subtract: (i) $\frac{7}{9} - \frac{7}{13}$ (ii) $\frac{11}{13} - \frac{3}{7}$ (iii) $\frac{8}{9} - \frac{5}{8}$ (iv) $\frac{8}{13} - \frac{3}{5}$ (v) $\frac{6}{13} - \frac{1}{11}$

For improper fractions:

Example: Subtract: $\frac{21}{5} - \frac{37}{11} = \frac{21*11-37*5}{5*11} = \frac{46}{55}$.

Practice Exercise: Subtract: (i) $\frac{14}{9} - \frac{17}{13}$ (ii) $\frac{11}{3} - \frac{23}{7}$ (iii) $\frac{42}{9} - \frac{35}{8}$ (iv) $\frac{38}{13} - \frac{13}{5}$

For mixed fractions: Here, the whole number parts of both numbers are subtracted and the fraction parts are subtracted separately.

Example: Subtract: $8\frac{3}{5} - 6\frac{2}{7} = (8-6) + (\frac{3*7-2*5}{5*7}) = 2\frac{11}{35}$

Practice Exercise: Subtract: (i) $5\frac{4}{7} - 2\frac{3}{8}$ (ii) $9\frac{3}{4} - 3\frac{1}{6}$ (iii) $16\frac{4}{7} - 8\frac{2}{9}$

c) **Multiplication:** In this process, the numerators are multiplied together and the denominators are multiplied. The new fraction is the product of numerators ÷ by the product of the denominators. It can be represented as:

$$\frac{a}{b} \times \frac{c}{d} = \frac{ac}{bd}$$

For proper and improper fractions:

Example: (i) $\frac{4}{7} \times \frac{3}{5} = \frac{12}{35}$ (ii) $\frac{14}{9} \times \frac{11}{7} = \frac{154}{63}$

For mixed fractions: Multiply the whole numbers separately and the fractions separately.

Example: $3\frac{5}{9} \times 8\frac{3}{7} = 24\frac{5}{21}$

Practice Exercise: Solve: (i) $\frac{14}{17} \times \frac{13}{24}$ (ii) $\frac{21}{23} \times \frac{12}{13}$ (iii) $\frac{13}{5} \times \frac{12}{7}$
(iv) $\frac{35}{11} \times \frac{41}{12}$
(v) $9\frac{2}{9} \times 4\frac{3}{7}$ (vi) $15\frac{6}{7} \times 12\frac{8}{13}$

d) **Division:** This operation is carried out by multiplying the first fraction with the transposed or inverted second fraction. It can be represented as :

$$\frac{a}{b} \div \frac{c}{d} = \frac{a}{b} \times \frac{d}{c} = \frac{ad}{bc}$$

For mixed fractions→ convert the same to improper fractions and then calculate.

Example: (i) $\frac{4}{9} \div \frac{3}{8} = \frac{32}{27}$ (ii) $\frac{21}{5} \div \frac{11}{6} = \frac{126}{55}$ (iii) $5\frac{3}{7} \div 2\frac{7}{8} = \frac{38}{7} \div \frac{23}{8} = \frac{304}{161} = 1\frac{143}{161}$.

Practice Exercises: (i) $\frac{6}{11} \div \frac{5}{7}$ (ii) $\frac{9}{7} \div \frac{7}{8}$ (iii) $\frac{14}{9} \div \frac{15}{8}$ (iv) $9\frac{5}{7} \div 4\frac{7}{9}$ (v) $7\frac{2}{5} \div 3\frac{5}{6}$

D. Converting fractions to decimals:

To convert a fraction to its decimal form we divide the numerator by the denominator.

Examples: (i) $\frac{1}{2} = 0.5$ (ii) $\frac{1}{3} = 0.333333...$ (iii) $\frac{1}{4} = 0.25$ (iv) $\frac{1}{5} = 0.20$ (v) $\frac{1}{6} = 0.16666...$
(vi) $\frac{1}{7} = 0.142857142857...$ (vii) $\frac{1}{8} = 0.125$ (viii) $\frac{1}{9} = 0.1111...$

From the above examples of finding decimals of fractions with denominators from 2 to 9, we can see that

a) 2, 4, 5 and 8 divided the numerator 1 completely. The decimal values did not repeat themselves, hence they are called **non-recurring decimals**.

b) While 3 and 9 gave a decimal value that repeats itself endlessly and the number 7 gave a set of 6 decimal values that repeated itself, so these are called **recurring decimals**. They are denoted by a dot on top of the recurring number or a dot on the first and last recurring digits of a recurring set.

c) The number 6, however, gave us 1 non-recurring and 1 recurring value. This is a **partial recurring decimal.**

Some important observations:

(i) When the denominator of a fraction contains only 2 and 5 as factors, we get non-recurring decimal, with each 2, 5 or10 giving one significant digit to the decimal. For e.g.

$\frac{1}{2} = 0.5$, $\frac{1}{4} = \frac{1}{2\times2} = 0.25$, $\frac{1}{5} = 0.2$, $\frac{1}{25} = \frac{1}{5\times5}$ =0.04, $\frac{1}{40} = \frac{1}{2\times2\times10}$ =0.025.

Denominators consisting of 3, 7, 9, 11 or higher prime numbers as factors and no 2, or 5, will give us recurring decimals. Each 3 or 9 will give only 1 recurring digit, 11 contributes 2 and 7 gives a set of 6 recurring digits

.

(ii) For each non-recurring decimal of a fraction having its numerator as 1, when the last digit of the denominator is multiplied with the last digit of the decimal, the product will always end in a 0.

When the last recurring digit of the recurring decimal set of a fraction with 1 as its numerator is multiplied with its divisor/denominator, the last digit of the product is 9.

This is helpful in determining, beforehand, the last digit of the denominator of the fraction.

For e.g. 2 x 0.5 = 1, $0.\dot{3}$ (1 repeating digit) x 3 = 0.9, 0.125 x 8 = 1.0, 0.2 x 5 = 1.0 ,
$0.\dot{1}4285\dot{7}$ x 7 = 7(last digit of recurring set) x7 = 49 and $0.\dot{1}$ x 9 = 0.9.

E. Properties of Recurring Decimals:

(i) In the division process of converting a fraction, often called a vulgar fraction, to its decimal form, each step gives us a remainder. All the **remainders are said to be in Geometric Progression (G.P.)**. This fact makes it extremely simple and helps to avoid
long division steps. Let us take the example of $\frac{1}{7}$.

```
7 | 1.0  | 0.142857
    7
    30
    28
     20
     14
      60
      56
       40
       35
        50
        49
         1
```

The division gives remainders 1, 3, 2, 6, 4, 5 and 1 again. Taking the first 2 remainders we can say the G.P. = 1 : 3. Moving to the third, the remainder should be 3 x 3 = 9. Since 9 > 7, so 9-7 = 2, the 3rd remainder. The 4th = 2x3 =6. Then the 5th = 6 x 3 = 18 – 14 =4 and the 6th = 4 x 3 = 12-7=5. Hence, we can say that the remainders are in G.P. This saves us the unnecessary division steps as if we have the G.P. of the first 2 remainders, we can easily calculate the rest of the remainders. This is specially useful for dividing large denominators. Another method of finding the remainders is to add a 0 to 3 and divide by 7to give 2 as the R. Adding a 0 to the 2 and 20÷7→R = 6, 60÷7→R = 4 and 40÷7→R =5.

(ii) Another advantage of being able to calculate the remainders is that they can be divided mentally **to get the quotient digits easily and quickly**. Hence, 1, 3, 2, 6, 4, 5 taken as 10, 30, 20, 60, 40 and 50 when divided by 7 will give us 142857 as the recurring decimal set in a jiffy.

There is an even more quicker method based on the ***Sheshyankena Charmena*** sutra meaning *'the remainders by the last digit'*. Here, the division is done away with completely. We place not the dividend- nucleus digits but the remainder digits themselves in order. So we take 3, 2, 6, 4, 5, 1 and multiply each digit from the left by 7 and put down only the last digit of the product as the Q digit. So, in 3 x 7 = 21, we take only 1 as the first Q digit. Similarly, 7 x 2 = 4, 7 x 6 = 2, 7 x 4 = 8,7 x 5 = 5 and 7 x 1 = 7. Hence this transformed product will be 142857.

(iii) If the **last digit of the denominator of a fraction is 9** and the numerator 1, we can safely say that the last digit of the decimal is 1. This is important as in the division process one works with these fractions, using the ***Ekadhikena*** sutra. For denominators ending in 1, 3, and 7, the fractions can be converted to ones with last digit 9 in denominators by multiplying with 9, 3 and 7 respectively.

The Vedic sutras have given some special upasutras with a few sample-specimens which along with the ***Ekanyunena*** Sutra help in postulating mental one-line solutions to the problem. The 3 samples are:

(a) ***Kevalaih Saptakam Gunayat:*** translates as 'for 7 multiplicand is 143'. 'Saptaka' stands for 7 and 'Kevalaih' for 143.

It means that for denominator 7, the decimal values will be 143 x 999 = 142 | 857.

(b) ***Kalau Kshudrasasaih:*** Here 'Kalau' means 13 and 'Kshudrasasaih' represents '077'.

So, for denominator13, the decimal will be = 077 x 999 = 076 | 923

(c) ***Kamse Kshamadaaha-khalairmalaih:*** states that for 17 multiplicand is 05882353.

So, 17 being the denominator, decimal = 05882353 x 999 = 05882352 | 94117647.

The above results may be formulated as:

$$\frac{1}{7} = \frac{143x999}{999999} = \frac{142857}{999999} = 0.142857$$

$$\frac{1}{13} = \frac{077\times999}{999999} = \frac{076923}{999999} = 0.076923$$

$$\frac{1}{17} = \frac{05882353\times99999999}{9999999999999999} = \frac{0588235294117647}{9999999999999999} = 0.588235294117647$$

Also, on cross multiplying, we get 7 x 142857 = 9999999, 13 x 076923 = 999999. The fact that for fractions with 1 as numerator as 1 and last digit of denominator being 1, 3, 7 or 9 will have as its decimal last digit as 9, 3, 7 and 1 respectively.

(iv) Another important property is the **R digits and Q digits complements cycle**. Here, two halves of the Q digits set, when added together give us a series of 9s, while the sum of the two halves of R digits will give us a series of the divisor number. Hence we can conclude that the second half of the Q digits are complements from 9, of the first half, while the second half of the R digits are complements from the divisor, of the first half.

For e.g. R digits of the above example = 3, 2, 6, 4, 5,1.
Sum of two halves = 3,2,6 + 4,5,1 = 7, 7, 7
Q digits = 1 4 2 8 5 7 and
Sum of the two halves = 1 4 2 + 8 5 7 = 9 9 9 9 9 9.

(v) **Multiples of basic fractions:** So far we have taken the numerator to be 1. For other values of the numerator, the basic decimal will alter accordingly. Let us take $\frac{1}{7}$ again as an example:

$\frac{1}{7} = 0.142857$, $\frac{2}{7} = 0.285714$, $\frac{3}{7} = 0.428571$, $\frac{4}{7} = 0.571428$, $\frac{5}{7} = 0.714285$, $\frac{6}{7} = 0.857142$

In the example above, the values of the numerator increase by 1. The value of the decimal also changes. But the special observation is that the decimal values moves accordingly in the same direction with the same digits. That is the reason this division is called 'cyclic'. There are 3 ways to look at the other divisions:

(a) The first numerator 1 gives a Q digit of 1 in the first place, numerator as 2, gives 2 as the first digit, since there is no 3 in the decimal then the numerator 3 will give a decimal starting with 4 and so on.

(b) Multiplying the numerator and denominator gives a product whose last digit is the same as the last digit of the decimal. For e.g. 7 x 2 = 14 and last digit of decimal is 4 which is equal to the last digit of the product.

(c) When numerator is 1, the decimal begins with 0.14. Then with 2 as the numerator, the decimal should begin with 0.14 x 2 = 0.28, with 3, decimal = 0.14 x 3 = 0.42 and so on.

In the Modern Mathematics system, the smaller denominators may divide the numerator easily. The problem arises when the denominators get bigger and the division process becomes very complicated and lengthy. This method is simplified to a great extent by the principles of Vedic mathematics. Here, the vulgar fraction is converted to an 'auxiliary' fraction.

F. The Auxiliary Fraction (A.F):

This type of fraction is called the '***Sahayak***' or '*assistant*' fraction and makes the complicated divisions easier. There are 2 types of auxiliary fractions;

Type 1:

The first type adopts the ***Ekadhikena*** Sutra to simplify the divisor. The fraction has to have a denominator ending in 9. Then the digits before the 9 are increased by 1 to give the modified divisor/multiplier. The division is carried out from the left and instead of carrying over the remainder to the next 0, we prefix it to its quotient digit to get the next dividend. The division continues in this way till the digits start repeating themselves.

One can even use a multiplication process. Since the denominator ends in 9, then the last digit of the recurring set will end in 1. Therefore, we put 1 down as the last digit of the set to the extreme right and multiplying each digit from the right we prefix the remainder to be carried over, do the addition and keep multiplying till we get to the first digit.

For e.g. Fraction (F) $=\frac{1}{19}$, then the A.F = $\frac{0.1}{2}$ and

By division: $\frac{0.1}{2} = 0._{1}\dot{0}_{0}5_{1}2_{0}6_{0}3_{1}1_{1}5_{1}7_{1}8 \mid 94736842\dot{1}$

In the division above, the number of decimal digits (n) = D – 1 = 18. Also the half mark of the set is = D – N = 18. When we reached the dividend of 18 on the 9th digit, we stopped dividing further and took the complement from 9 for every digit from the decimal point moving left. The 18 digit decimal ends in 1 and repeats the set on further division.

By multiplication: $\frac{0.1}{2} = 0.\dot{0}52631578 \mid 9^{1}47^{1}3^{1}6842\dot{1}$

As discussed before, for this method we place the last digit of the set (1 in this case) to the extreme right and multiply it by 2. We place the product to the left of this digit. This becomes the new multiplicand. We continue leftward in this manner, adding all the carrying numbers to the new product till we again reach the ninth digit and put down the complement from 9 for each digit from right to left.

Sometimes, the **denominator may have more than one 9**. For e.g. $\frac{52}{499}, \frac{132}{3999}$ & $\frac{21863}{29999}$ are fractions having 2, 3 and 4 nines in their denominator. The method to convert these will follow the previous one with one slight difference. The dividend will be grouped as per the number of nines. Hence, the above fractions will have the numerator digits grouped by 2, 3 and 4 digits and the final remainder will be as usual prefixed to the group and becomes the first digit of the next dividend group.

Example: F = $\frac{52}{499}$, then A.F = $\frac{0.52}{5}$ dividend to be grouped by 2 digits as two 9s.

$\therefore \frac{0.52}{5} =$

$0.{}_{2}10_{0}42_{2}08_{3}41_{1}68_{3}33_{3}66_{1}73_{3}34_{4}66_{1}93_{3}38_{3}67_{2}73_{3}54_{4}70_{0}94_{4}$
$18_{3}83_{3}76_{1}75_{0}35 \mid$

${}_{0}07_{2}01_{1}40_{0}28_{3}01_{1}60_{0}32_{2}06_{1}41_{1}28_{3}25_{0}65_{0}13_{3}02_{2}60_{0}52_{\mathbf{2}}\mathbf{10}$**...**(repeating)

$= 0.\dot{1}04208416833667334669338677354709418837675350701402801603206412825651302605\dot{2}$

If the **denominator ends in 3 or 7** instead of 9, we multiply the fraction by 3 and 7 respectively, to convert it to a fraction with denominator ending with 9.

For e.g. F= $\frac{1}{17}$, then A.F = $\frac{1\times7}{7\times7} = \frac{7}{49} = \frac{0.7}{5}$. The rest of the method remains the same.

For denominators ending in 8, 7, 6, the method is again a little different. Since they are 1, 2 and 3 less than 9, then on solving, after dividing the nucleus digit, the quotient is added once, twice and thrice to the quotient and to get the new dividend. The ***Anurupyena*** upasutra comes into use here.

Example: F = $\frac{15}{68}$, A.F = $\frac{1.5}{7}$ since 68 is 1 less than 69, then 1 quotient digit is added to the dividend every time.

$\therefore \frac{1.5}{7} =$

$0.{}_{1}2_{0}2_{4}0_{5}5_{4}8_{0}8_{2}2_{3}3_{1}5_{6}2_{1}9_{0}4_{1}1_{5}1_{3}7_{2}6_{4}4_{6}6_{0}\mathbf{8}_{2}\mathbf{2}_{3}\mathbf{3}$...(repeating)

$= 0.220558\dot{\mathbf{8}}\mathbf{23529411764}\dot{\mathbf{6}}$

Dividing 1.5 by 7 we get Q =0.2 and R =1. The dividend then becomes 12 (prefixing the R digit to the Q digit). Adding 1 quotient digit to this we get the dividend as 12 +2 =14. Dividing in this way continuously results in a non-recurring set of 0.220558 and a recurring set of 8235294117646.

Type 2:

This type of Auxiliary fraction is used when the actual fraction has a denominator that ends in 1. While converting, the 1 in the denominator is dropped, keeping the rest of the number as divisor and the numerator is reduced by 1 (***Ekanyunena***). The division is like the previous method. The difference is that each quotient digit is converted to its complement from 9 and along with the remainder prefixed, is the modified dividend.

Example: F = $\frac{1}{31}$, then A.F = $\frac{0.0}{3}$ and

$$\frac{0.0}{3} = 0._{0}0_{0}3_{0}2_{1}2_{2}5_{0}8_{1}0_{1}6_{1}4_{0}5_{1}1_{0}6_{0}1_{2}2_{0}9 = 0.\dot{0}3225806451612\dot{9}$$

.

In the division above, we divide 0.0 by 3 to get Q = .0 and R = 0. Taking the complement of the Q digit from 9 and prefixing the R digit to this number gives us the next dividend which, in this case is 09. Dividing this by 3, we get Q = 3 and R = 0, so the next dividend = 06. We continue to divide in this manner till we get the last recurring digit.

Fractions with denominators ending in 01, 001, 0001 will be divided by grouping the dividend into sets of 2, 3 or 4 digits. Divide this set by the divisor fully, prefix the final remainder to the front of the quotient set that has been converted to its complements from 9 and divide the new set again.

G. Converting decimals into fractions:

For non-recurring decimals:

These are converted be dividing the decimal set by 10^n where n = number of digits after the decimal point.
For e.g. $0.5 = \frac{5}{10} = \frac{1}{2}$, $0.25 = \frac{25}{100} = \frac{1}{4}$, $0.025 = \frac{25}{1000} = \frac{1}{40}$.

For partly recurring decimals: There are 2 methods:

(i) Take a variable as the value of the decimal. The first 10's multiple of the variable should be equal to the number of non-recurring decimal digits. The second 10's multiple should be equal to the total non-recurring and recurring digits. Subtracting the former from the latter will enable us to remove the decimal part. The difference is then divided by the difference of the variables to arrive at the actual fraction.

(ii) Take the entire non-recurring with the recurring digits. Subtract the non- recurring digits from this number. Divide the difference by the product of 10s amounting to the non-recurring digits and 9s equalling the number of recurring digits. This will give the needed fraction.

Example: a) Convert 0.16666 to fraction.

(i)Let x = 0.1666666. 1 is the non- recurring and 6 is the recurring digit.
Then 10x = 1.6666… and 100x = 16.6666…..
Subtracting, 100x – 10x = 16.6666 – 1.66666 → 90x = 15.
Therefore, $x = \frac{15}{90} = \frac{1}{6}$.

(ii) $0.1\dot{6} = (16 - 1) / (10 \times 9) = \frac{15}{90} = \frac{1}{6}$.

b) Convert $2.25\dot{3}$ to its fraction form. → 2 + 0.253333

(i) Let x = 0.253333, then 100x = 25.33333.. and 1000x = 253.3333.
Therefore, 1000x – 100x = 253.333 -25.333 = 228 and x = 2 + (228/900) = $2\frac{19}{75}$.
(ii) 2 + 0.253333 = 2 + (253 – 25)/ 100 x 9 = $2\frac{19}{75}$.

For recurring decimals:

(i) Use the variable method as above or

(ii) Divide the decimal by the same number of 9s as there are digits in the decimal.

For e.g. $0.\dot{1}4285\dot{7}$ →(i) Let x = 0.142857142857, then 1000000x = 142857.1428571428..

Therefore, 1000000x – x = 999999x = 142857. $x = \frac{142857}{999999} = \frac{1}{7}$.
(ii) $\frac{142857}{999999} = \frac{1}{7}$.

Practice Exercise: Convert to fraction: (i) 0.225 (ii) 2.07 (iii) $0.\dot{0}\dot{9}$ (iv) $3.45\dot{3}\dot{9}$ (v) $7.\dot{0}7692\dot{3}$

Chapter 9.

VARGA /SQUARES

Squares, here, does not mean the 4 sided figures but is taken as a verb. Squaring a number means to multiply it once more by itself for e.g. $5^2 = 5*5 = 25$. The superscript of 2 over 5 reads as '5 squared'. The table included below lists the squared numbers from 1 to 30:

Number	Squared	Number	Squared	Number	Squared
1	1	11	121	21	441
2	4	12	144	22	484
3	9	13	169	23	529
4	16	14	196	24	576
5	25	15	225	25	625
6	36	16	256	26	676
7	49	17	289	27	729
8	64	18	324	28	784
9	81	19	361	29	841
10	100	20	400	30	900

In case the squaring of the numbers from 11 to 30 are difficult to remember, the student can create this table in the following manner:

Starting from 11, which is 1 more than the base number 10, we add this deficiency/ excess to 11and keep to the left side of the product and put 1^2 to the right. This gives the final product as 121. Similarly, $12^2 = (12 + 2) | 2^2 = 144$, $13^2 = (13 + 3) | 3^2 = 169$ and so on.

When the number moves away from the base and is nearer to its sub-base, the upasutra **Anurupyena** or '*proportionately*' comes into use. For 21^2, we consider the sub-base 20 (10*2), consider the first deviation from this base as + 1, add this deviation to 21, multiply the sum by 2,proportionately, and put this product on the left side and the square of +1 on the right. Hence, $21^2 = 2(21 + 1) | 1^2 = 441$, $22^2 = 2(22 + 2) | 2^2 = 484$. If the right hand side product is a 2 digit number, carry the tens place number to the left side. For e.g. $14^2 = (14 + 4) | 4^2 = 18 | 16 = 196$.

Remember: a) The number of digit places to be kept on the right side is equal to the number of 0s in the base number. In this case, there is only one 0 in the base 10. Therefore, there will be only the unit digit of the square kept on the right side and the excess is to be carried over to the left side.

b) For all subsequent squaring say, 31 – 39, 41 -49 etc, the sub-bases viz. 30, 40 etc are to be taken and calculated accordingly. Also, the multiple of the base is to be applied only on the left hand side of the calculation.

Squaring numbers from 30 to 70 is done by taking the base as 50, subtracting the number to be squared from 25 and this difference to be kept on the left hand side while the square of the deviation is kept (only the unit and tens digits) on the right. For squaring say, 46, the deviation from 50 is -4. Hence $46^2 = (46 - 25) | (-4)^2 = 21 | 16 = 2116$. In this case since the subbase is 50 it is considered as ½ *100, therefore there will be 2 digit places for the right side as 100 has two 0s.

a) The Base method: Uses the Sutra ***Nikhilam*** and its Upasutra ***Yaavadunam Taavadunikritya Varga Cha Yojayet*** which translates into '*Whatever the deficiency, lessen/ increase by that amount and set up the square of the deficiency*'. This is useful while squaring 2-digit, 3-digit, 4-digit etc. numbers that are close to their base.

Example:

Squaring a number close to base 100:

- To square 97, the deficiency or deviation (d) = 97 -100 = -3. So, $97^2 = 97 - 3 \mid 3^2 = 9409$.

-To square 104, (d) = + 4. Hence, $104^2 = 104 + 4 \mid 4^2 = 10816$.

- Squaring a number close to 1000: (3digit places on the right side)

To square 994, (d) = -6, and $994^2 = 994 - 6 \mid (-6)^2 = 988036$.

To square 1003, (d) = + 3 and $1003^2 = 1003 + 3 \mid 3^2 = 1006009$.

- Squaring a number close to 10000:

- $9999^2 = 9998 \mid 0001$
- $10004^2 = 10008 \mid 0016$

Practice Exercises: Find : a) 87^2 b) 113^2 c) 996^2 d) 1007^2 e) 99991^2 f) 9999873^2

b) The Duplex method: or the *Dvandva Yog Vidhi* uses the formula of squaring of numbers. For example, while squaring a 2 digit number say 'ab' we consider the formula $(a + b)^2 = a^2 + 2ab + b^2$. The only difference is that we replace the addition sign by the balancing bar and reach the value of the product after balancing the numbers in the partitions. So, $28^2 = 2^2 \mid 2*2*8 \mid 8^2 = 4 \mid 32 \mid 64 = 784$.

This formula method works with smaller numbers. For squaring larger numbers we will use the duplex method.(refer Special Methods). To solve, we take the duplex (D) of subsequent numbers. Let us take an example of a 4 digit number ‘abcd’. Then

$(abcd)^2 = D(a) \mid D(ab) \mid D(abc) \mid D(abcd) \mid D(bcd) \mid D(cd) \mid D(d)$.

To recall,

- $D(a) = a^2$
- $D(ab) = 2ab$
- $D(abc) = 2ac + b^2$
- $D(abcd) = 2ad + 2bc$
- $D(bcd) = 2bd + c^2$
- $D(cd) = 2cd$
- $D(d) = d^2$

Let us try some actual examples:

- For a 2 digit number say 46,
  $46^2 = D(4) \mid D(46) \mid D(6) = 4^2 \mid 2*4*6 \mid 6^2 = 16 \mid 48 \mid 36 =$ 2116.

- For a 3 digit number say, 543,
  $543^2 = 5^2 \mid 2*5*4 \mid 2*5*3 + 4^2 \mid 2*4*3 \mid 3^2 = 25|40|46|24|9$
  $= 294849$

- For a 4 digit number, say, 1234
  $1234^2 = 1^2|2*1*2|2*1*3 + 2^2|2*1*4 + 2*2*3|2*2*4 + 3^2|2*3*4|4^2$
  $= 1 \mid 4 \mid 10 \mid 20 \mid 25 \mid 24 \mid 16 = 1522756$.

The above method looks complicated now but with ample practice, one can do the squaring mentally from left to right in a matter of minutes.

Practice : Find the squares by duplex method of **a) 29 b) 84 c) 99 d) 126 e) 387 f) 763 g) 885 h) 905 i) 2567 j) 4678 k) 7865 l) 9898 m) 12345**.

Some special cases:

1. Squaring numbers ending with '5': Like the rule followed for multiplication of 2 number where the unit digits of both numbers added up to 10 and all other digits being the same, one multiplies the unit digits for the rightmost product and the rest of the number by 1 more (**Ekadhikena**) than the number. The same is done here in squaring a number ending with 5, since 5 + 5 =10 in the units place and the rest of the number being identical.

So, $15^2 = 1*(1+1) \mid 5^2 = 225$, $25^2 = 2*3 \mid 25 = 625$, $115^2 = 11*12 \mid 25 = 13225$.

The rightmost 2 digits will always be 25 and the left side will be the product of the rest of the number and 1 more than that number.

2. Squaring 3 digit numbers having '0' as the tens place number: The method to solve such a number is to first square the hundreds digit then to multiply the first and last digit and double it and finally square the unit number. The units and tens number will have 2 digit places as base is 100.

For e.g. $103^2 = 1^2 \mid 1*3*2 \mid 3^2 = 1 \mid 06 \mid 09 = 10609$.

$206^2 = 2^2 \mid 2*6*2 \mid 6^2 = 4 \mid 24 \mid 36 = 42436$.

$808^2 = 8^2 \mid 8*8*2 \mid 8^2 = 64 \mid 128 \mid 64 = 652864$ (as tens place only 2 digits)

3. The Arthur Benjamin formula for squaring: Dr.Arthur Benjamin put forth a formula for easy squaring based on the base method. He stated that:

$$\mathbf{A^2 = (A + d)(A - d) + d^2}$$

where A is the number to be squared and 'd' is the deviation of the number from its nearest base. He proposed that the number moves up or down to the nearest base or sub-base, then moves back just as much in the other direction. For example in squaring 98, the number moves up +2 to 100 and back -2 to (98 – 2 =) 96.

Using the formula then,

$98^2 = (98 + 2)(98 - 2) + 2^2 = 100*96 + 4 = 9604$.

There are many methods to square a number. It is up to the discretion of the student to solve the same. In doing so, one can develop excellent concentration, observation and decision making skills.

Practice Exercises: Find a) 35^2 b) 145^2 c) 235^2 d) 125^2 e) 645^2 f) 209^2 g) 304^2 h) 708^2 i) 903^2 j) 807^2 and by formula: k) 89^2 l) 68^2 m) 59^2 n) 99^2 o) 82^2

Chapter 10.

VARGAMULA /SQUARE ROOTS

When a number is squared, the number is considered the root of the squared number. For e.g. in $5^2 = 25$, 5 is the root of 25. Finding the square root of a number is the reverse of squaring a number. The squared number may be a perfect square or an imperfect square. A perfect square results in a whole positive number while an imperfect square yields a decimal number. The square root of a number is denoted by '$\sqrt{}$' or $()^{1/2}$. Hence, $\sqrt{25} = 5$ or $(25)^{1/2} = 5$.

1. Finding the square root of a perfect square:

(a) By the Vilokanam / observation method:

Number	Squared	Number	Squared	Number	Squared
1	**1**	11	**121**	21	**441**
2	**4**	12	**144**	22	**484**
3	**9**	13	**169**	23	**529**
4	**16**	14	**196**	24	**576**
5	**25**	15	**225**	25	**625**
6	**36**	16	**256**	26	**676**
7	**49**	17	**289**	27	**729**
8	**64**	18	**324**	28	**784**
9	**81**	19	**361**	29	**841**
10	**100**	20	**400**	30	**900**

Observing the table above, we see that the squared numbers end in 0, 1, 4, 5, 6 & 9 only. Hence, numbers ending in 2, 3, 7 & 8 are **NOT** perfect squares. The numbers ending in 0, 1, 4 , 5, 6 & 9 are not always necessarily perfect squares but generally perfect squares always end in those numbers. Therefore, while calculating square roots we can see the following:

Squared nos. ending with	**Square roots end with**
0	**0**
1	**1 or 9**
4	**2 or 8**
5	**5**
6	**4 or 6**
9	**3 or 7**

Let us solve some problems with this method:

i) Find the square root of 676.

The last digit is 6, hence the square root number will end in either 4 or 6. The number has to grouped with 2 digits from the right. So, the groups will be 6 & 76. The number of groups denotes the number of digits (n) in the answer. Here, n = 2 as there are 2 groups and the last digit could be either 4 or 6. Taking the first group, the nearest perfect square to 6 is between 4 and 9 or 2^2 and 3^2 or 2 and 3. We take the smaller root in this case which is 2. Therefore the square root could be either 24 or 26. To check the correct answer we could either:
- multiply 2 * 3 = 6 = 6 (ambiguous answer) or
- take the square of the average of the numbers i.e. $25^2 = 625 < 676$. Since the number is higher than 25^2 we take the greater number i.e. 26 So, $\sqrt{\mathbf{676}} = \mathbf{26}$.

ii) $\sqrt{6084} = ?$

Grouping from right we have 2 groups of 60 and 84 respectively, hence answer is a 2 digit number. Last digit denotes that the last digit of answer will be either a 2 or an 8. The first group root lies between 7 and 8. Hence the two possible answers are 72 and 78 but $75^2 = 5625 < 6084$. Therefore, $\sqrt{\mathbf{6084}} = \mathbf{78}$

(b) By division with duplex method:

Solving by mere observation is easier with small numbers. To solve larger perfect squares we use division with the duplex method. After grouping, the first digit pair is considered as 'a^2' [D(a)] and the nearest root as 'a'. We then start dividing the rest of the numbers with '2a'[D(ab) = 2ab] to find 'b' and so on. The duplex of the quotient number starts after the first division [D(b)] only. The duplex number is consecutively subtracted from the modified dividend and the difference is divided by the divisor 2a. the following examples will elucidate the same.

i) $\sqrt{19321}$ = ? n = 3, groups = 1 93 21

$$
\begin{array}{llllll}
 & (a^2) & & & & \\
2 & 1 & {}^{0}9 & {}^{3}3 & {}^{6}2 & {}^{8}1 \text{ – superscript = remainder.}
\end{array}
$$

$$
\begin{array}{rrrrrrl}
(2a) & & - & -9 & -54 & -81 & \\
 & & 9 & 24 & 08 & 0 & \\
 & 1 & 6 & 18 & 0 & 0 & \\
\hline
\mathbf{1} & \mathbf{3} & \mathbf{9.} & 0 & 0 & & n = 3 \\
(a) & & & -D(3) & -D(39) & -D(390) &
\end{array}
$$

So, $\sqrt{\mathbf{19321}}$ = **139.**

ii) $\sqrt{226576}$ = ? n = 3, groups = 22 65 76

$$
\begin{array}{rrrrrrr}
8 & 22 & {}^{6}6 & {}^{10}5 & {}^{8}7 & {}^{3}6 & \\
 & & & - & -49 & -84 & -36 \\
 & 66 & 56 & 03 & 0 & & \\
 & 16 & 56 & 48 & 0 & 0 & \\
\hline
 & \mathbf{4} & \mathbf{7} & \mathbf{6.} & 0 & 0 &
\end{array}
$$

So, $\sqrt{\mathbf{226576}}$ = **476.**

2. Finding square root of an imperfect square: The square root of an imperfect number will result in a decimal number. The same division method is used for both imperfect and decimal numbers.

a) $\sqrt{35}$ =? n = 1 , only 1 group of 2 digits.

10	35	$^{10}0$	$^{10}0$	$^{9}0$	$^{12}0$	$^{11}0$	$^{28}0$
		-	-81	-18	-109	- 12	-162
		100	19	72	11	98	118…..
	25	90	10	60	0	70	.
	5.	9	1	6	0	7……..	

∴ $\mathbf{\sqrt{35} = 5.91607}$ ...

b)$\sqrt{6558}$ =? n = 2, groups = 65 58.

16	65	$^{1}5$	$^{15}8$	$^{14}0$	$^{12}0$	$^{23}0$	$^{22}0$
		-	-0	-0	-81	-144	- 82
		15	158	140	39	86	130….
	64	0	144	128	16	64	.
	8	0.	9	8	1	4…..	

∴ $\mathbf{\sqrt{6558} = 80.9814}$ ...

3. Finding square root of a decimal number: When working with a decimal number, the grouping for the whole numbers is done from right to left from the decimal point , while the decimal part is grouped in twos from left to the right after the decimal point.

a) $\sqrt{0.2634}$ =? n = 0 groups = 00 . 26 34

10	0.	26	$^{1}3$	$^{3}4$	$^{3}0$	$^{4}0$	$^{7}0$
			-	-1	-6	-13	-16
			13	33	24	27	54.....
		25	10	30	20	20	.
	0.	5	1	3	2	2.....	

∴ $\sqrt{\mathbf{0.2634}} = \mathbf{0.51322}$ ...

b) $\sqrt{11.6213}$ = ? n = 1, groups = 11 62 13

6	11.	26	$^{2}2$	$^{6}1$	$^{7}3$	$^{1}0$	$^{10}0$	$^{7}0$
		-	-16	-0	-72	-0	-81	-16
		26	6	61	1	10	19	54....
	9	24	0	54	0	0	12	.
	3.	4	0	9	0	0	2.....	

∴ $\sqrt{\mathbf{11.6213}} = \mathbf{3.409002}$ ...

An important point to remember while dividing the number is to carefully select the quotient number. If the remainder of the division is less than the duplex number to be deducted, then we get a negative modified dividend. In such a case, reduce the quotient by an appropriate value so that it is greater than the duplex number to facilitate the division process.

Practice Exercises: Find the square root of the following:

a) 4356 b) 2209 c) 5184 d) 6889 e) 9316 f) 20164 g) 36864
h) 512656 i) 155236 j) 799236 k) 4.6612 l) 157.9546
m) 33.2709 n) 0.07236

Chapter 11.

GHANAAKAR / CUBES

Not referring to the solid figure, cubing a number means to multiply the same number two more times. A cube is denoted as '()3', hence, $3^3 = 3*3*3 = 27$. The operation reads as ' 3 cubed or 3 to the power 3 is 27' or '27 is a cube of 3'. The cubes from 1 to 10 are given in the following table:

Number	Cube	Number	Cube
1^3	1	6^3	216
2^3	8	7^3	343
3^3	27	8^3	512
4^3	64	9^3	729
5^3	125	10^3	1000

From the table above, one can observe that the cubes of the numbers 0, 1, 4, 5, 6 & 9 end in the same digit. The cubes of 2, 3, 7 and 8 end in 8, 7, 3 and 2 respectively, i.e. cube of 2 ends in 8 and cube of 3 ends in 7 and vice versa. The cube of a number can be calculated in various ways.

A. Formula method:

a) **Cubing a 2 digit number using the algebraic formula** $(a + b)^3 = a^3 + 3a^2b + 3ab^2 + b^3$. Considering the tens place digit of the number as 'a' and the unit digit as 'b' we can now rewrite the formula as $(ab)^3 = a^3 \mid 3a^2b \mid 3ab^2 \mid b^3$, replacing the '+' sign by balancing bars. The products are worked out as per the formula and then balanced accordingly to give the cube of the number. All numbers from 11 to 99 can be calculated easily this way.

- $14^3 = 1^3 | 3*1^2*4 | 3*1*4^2 | 4^3$ = 1 | 12 | 48 | 64 = 2744
- $27^3 = 2^3 | 3*2^2*7 | 3*2*7^2 | 7^3$ = 8 | 84 | 294 | 343 = 19683
- $81^3 = 8^3 | 3*8^2*1 | 3*8*1^2 | 1^3$ = 512 | 192 | 24 | 1 = 531441.

Some special cases :

- **Cubing a 2 digit number starting with 1**: In this case a =1 and b remains the same.
So, (1b)3 = 1 | 3b | 3b2 | b3. Therefore, $13^3 = 1 | 3*3 | 3* 3^2 | 3^3$ = 1 | 9 | 27 | 27 = 2197.

- **Cubing a 2 digit number ending with 1** will be calculated as (a1)3 = $a^3 | 3a^2 | 3a | 1$. Hence, $41^3 = 4^3 | 3*4^2 | 3*4 | 1$ = 64 | 48 | 12 | 1 = 68921.

- **Cubing a 2 digit number where both digits are the same** will be

$$(aa)^3 = a^3 | 3a^3 | 3a^3 | a^3.$$

So, $66^3 = 6^3 | 3*6^3 | 3*6^3 | 6^3$ = 216 | 648 | 648 | 216 = 287496.

b) **Cubing a smaller 3 digit number using the formula above** can be done by assuming the first 2 digits as ‘a’ and the last digit as ‘b’. While balancing, there will still be only 1 digit place in all partitions except the first one. An important observation is that cubing a 2 digit number will result in a cube with a minimum of 4 and maximum of 6 digits. A 3 digit number will give a minimum 7 digit cube.

- $106^3 = 10^3 | 3*10^2*6 | 3*10*6^2 | 6^3$ = 1000 | 1800 | 1080 | 216 = 1191016

c) **By Anurupyena (proportionately) method**. According to the sub-sutra a 2 digit number is calculated proportionately is

$$(ab)^3 = a^3 \mid a^2b \mid ab^2 \mid b^3$$
$$\mid +2a^2b \mid +2ab^2 \mid$$

and in the 2nd and 3rd partitions the number present is doubled and added to it. After balancing the same, we get the cube.

- $26^3 = 2^3 \mid 2^2*6 \mid 2*6^2 \mid 6^3 = 8 \mid 24 \mid 72 \mid 216 = 8 \mid 72 \mid 216 \mid 216 = 17576.$
$\mid +48 \mid +144 \mid$

d) **Cubing a larger 3 digit number** will use the following formula where the 3 digit are a, b and c respectively:

$$(abc)^3 = a^3 \mid 3a^2b \mid 3a(ac + b^2) \mid b^3 + 6abc \mid 3c(ac + b^2) \mid 3bc^2 \mid c^3$$

- $234^3 = 2^3 \mid 3*2^2*3 \mid 3*2(2*4 + 3^2) \mid 3^3 + 6*2*3*4 \mid 3*4(2*4 + 3^2) \mid 3*3*4^2 \mid 4^3$
$= 8 \mid 36 \mid 102 \mid 171 \mid 204 \mid 144 \mid 64 = 12812904$

* Note: when cubing a 3digit number there are, usually,7 partitions in the formula.

B. Base method:

When using the Nikhilam or Base method, the points to observe are the base (B), the deficiency/excess from B, called the deviation (D) and the new deviation (N) obtained after decreasing/increasing twice the deficiency(2D) from the number to be cubed. So, N = D +2D. The cubing is done by creating 3 spaces with digit places equal to the number of 0s in the base. The first space is calculated as (Number +/– 2D), the second as (N*D) and the third as D^3.

Therefore, **(Number)3 = Number (+/-) 2D | N x D | D^3.**
Number higher than base:

For a 2 digit number, say 13, B =10, D = +3, N =3 + 2*3 = 9 and

$13^3 = 13 + 6 \mid 9*3 \mid 3^3 = 19 \mid 27 \mid 27 = 2197$
(there will be only 1 digit place in the units and tens partitions as the base has only one 0.).

For a 3 digit number, say, 106, B = 100, D = +6, N = 18 and

$106^3 = 106 + 12 \mid 18 \times 6 \mid 216 = 118 \mid 108 \mid 216 = 1191016.$

For a 4 digit number, say, 1014, B = 1000, D = +14, N = 42 and

$1014^3 = 1014 + 28 \mid 42 \times 14 \mid 14^3 = 1042 \mid 588 \mid 2744 = 1042590744.$

Number lower than base:

For a 2 digit number say, 98. Then B = 100, D = -2, N = -6 and

$98^3 = 98 - 4 \mid -6 \times -2 \mid -2^3 = 94 \mid 12 \mid -08$(2 digit place) = 941192.

D^3 will give a vinculum or negative product. The excess digits are to be reduced from the next left part and then converted to a positive number (refer Vinculum Vidhi).

For a 3 digit number, say, 996, B = 1000, D = -4, N = -12 and

996^3 = 996 – 8 | -12 x -4 | -4^3 = 988 | 048 | -064 = 988047936.

For a 4 digit number say, 9987, B = 10000, D = -13, N = -39 and

9987^3 = 9987 – 26 | -39 x -13 | -13^3 = 9961 | 0507 | -2197 = 996105067803.

C. **Sub Base method:** Cubing numbers that are not close to their bases, but closer to their sub-bases (multiples of bases) will use the *Anurupyena* upasutra by cubing proportionately. In this case we first identify the true base (TB) of number to be cubed. Then identify the nearest sub-base (SB). Find the ratio M =TB/SB between the base and sub-base. The next step is to identify the deviation (D) from SB. Calculate the new deviation N = 3D. Thereafter, the cubing is done according to the following formula:

$(Number)^3 = M^2$(Number (+/-) 2D) | $3*M*D^2$ | D^3.

Number above a sub-base:

For a 2 digit number, say, 53, TB =10, SB = 50, M = 5, D = 3, N = 9 and

$53^3 = 5^2(53 + 6)$ | 3 x 5 x 3^2 | 3^3 = 1475 | 135 | 27 = 148877.

For a 3 digit number, say, 212, TB =100, SB = 200, M = 2, D =12, N = 36 and

212^3 = 4(212 + 24) | 3 x 2 x 144 | 12^3 = 944 | 864 | 1728 = 9528128.

For a 4 digit number, say 3008, TB = 1000, SB = 3000, M = 3, D = 8, N = 8 and

3008^3 = 9(3008 + 16) | 3 x 3 x 64 | 512 = 27216 | 576 | 512 = 27216576512.

Numbers below a sub-base:

For a 2 digit number, say, 47, TB =10, SB = 50, M = 5, D = -3, N = -27 and

47^3 = 25(47 – 6) | 3 x 5 x 9 | -27 = 1025 | 135 -2 | -7 = 103823.

For a 3 digit number, say, 387, TB =100, SB = 400, M = 4, D = -13, N = -39 and

387^3 = 16(387 – 26) | 3 x 4 x 169 | -2197 = 5776 | 2028 – 21 | -97 = 57960603.

All such numbers can be cubed easily with a little practice.

D. **Cubing a decimal number:** the first step is to ignore the decimal number and treat it as a whole number, cube the number and then put the decimal point at the required digit place.

For e.g. $(4.5)^3 = 45^3$ = 91125. Since there is only digit after the decimal point and since we are cubing the number, there will be 1 x 3 digits after the decimal point. Hence **$(4.5)^3$ = 91.125**.

For $(0.267)^3 = 267^3$ = 19034163. There will be 3*3 = 9 digits after the decimal. Therefore, **(0.267)3 = .019034163.**

Practice Exercises: Find the cubes of: (i) 24 (ii) 49 (iii) 74 (iv) 15 (v) 19 (vi) 61 (vii) 41 (viii) 88 (ix) 99 (x) 994 (xi) 982 (xii) 312 (xii) 4007 (xiv) 3.254.

Chapter 12.

GHANAMULA / CUBE ROOTS

When a number is cubed i.e. multiplied two times by itself, that number is called the cube root number of the cube. For e.g. In 3*3*3 = 27, 3 is the 'cube root' of 27 and 27 is the cube of 3.

Number	Cube	Number	Cube
1^3	1	6^3	216
2^3	8	7^3	343
3^3	27	8^3	512
4^3	64	9^3	729
5^3	125	10^3	1000

In the table above the cubes of numbers 1 to 10 are given. We can see that the cubes of 1, 4, 5, 6, 9 and 10 have the same end digit as the cube root. The cubes of 2, 3 7 & 8 end in 8, 7, 3 and 2 respectively.

Cube ends in:	Cube root ends in:
1	1
2	8
3	7
4	4
5	5
6	6
7	3
8	2
9	9
0	0

The table above is important when calculating the cube root of a number. Cubes are of 3 types, perfect, imperfect and decimal. Their cube roots will be whole numbers for perfect or exact cubes and decimal numbers for the imperfect and decimal cubes.

The preliminary process of finding the cube root (CR) of a number is to first create groups of 3digits of the number starting from the right. Each group represents a digit of the CR. The first group may or may not contain 3 digits.

For instance, to find the cube root of a)12167 and b) 328509, we take groups of 3 digits from the right. So the groups in the examples are a) 12 167 and b) 328 509 i.e. 2 groups apiece and number of digits (n) in each cube root will have n = 2 digits.

Cube Root methods:

1. By *Vilokanam*: or the observation method is the fastest and simplest way to find the cube root of a perfect cube having n = 2. Let us take the example from above:

a) $\sqrt[3]{12167} = ?$

The 2 groups are 12 and 167; n = 2
The first digit (F) and the last digit(L) can be mentally calculated.
For F, we take the perfect cube nearest to 12, in this case 8 (= 2^3). So **F = 2.**

For L, we see that the last digit of the group, 7 will have a cube root of 3 (refer table). So, **L = 3** and $\mathbf{\sqrt[3]{12167} = 23}$ **.**
b) $\sqrt[3]{328509} = ?$ Groups = 328 509, n = 2, F = 6 (216 nearest cube to 328) and L = 9 (last digit of cube is 9, so cube root will end in 9).

So, $\sqrt[3]{\mathbf{328509}} = \mathbf{69}$.
The above cubes have 2 groups only, so the solution becomes very easy for perfect cubes. For n= 3 or n = 4, a different method is used.

The formula for cubing a 3 digit number 'abc', is

$$\mathbf{a^3 \mid 3a^2b \mid 3ab^2 + 3a^2c \mid 6abc + b^3 \mid 3ac^2 + 3b^2c \mid 3bc^2 \mid c^3.}$$

For a 3 digit cube root, the advantage is that F and L are already determined for the perfect cube. We will now reverse the formula. The last group can be taken as 'a^3' and its cube root will give us 'a' or L, the units place digit.

The tens place digit(K) or 'b' is determined by subtracting L^3 from the right most digits of the cube. This removes the last digit and the difference obtained is calculated as $3L^2K(3a^2b)$. K or 'b' will be the multiple needed for $3L^2K$ to end as the last digit of the difference. This product is also subtracted to remove the penultimate digit of the cube.

The hundreds place(J) or 'c' is determined by $3L^2J + 3LK^2(3a^2c + 3ab^2)$. The extra number obtained as $3LK^2$ is first subtracted and the last digit of the difference will determine J as a multiple of $3L^2$. This calculation is not really required as here, J = F and has already been determined.

For n = 4, the same method is used for L, K and J. The thousandth place digit(H) here is F or 'd' but can be calculated, if required, as $3L^2H + 6LKJ + K^3$ $(3a^2d + 6abc + b^3)$ which is determined from $(L + K + J + H)^3$.

Examples: a) $\sqrt[3]{1601613}$ =?

On observation, groups = 1 601 613, n = 3, F = 1, L = 7. We have the first and last digit of the cube root. We now need to determine the tens place number(K).

CR of	1 601 613
For (L), L = 7, so L^3 = 343	343
	1 601 27
For (K), $3L^2K$ = 3*49* K = 147K(ends in 7) so K=1	1 47
	1 599 8
For (J), $3L^2J + 3LK^2$ = 147J + 21	-2 1
147J ends in 7 so J =1	1 597 7

We did not need to calculate J as F is already determined but just to cross-check we now see that the **CR of 1601613 = 117**.

b) $\sqrt[3]{76928302277}$ = ? groups = 76 928 302 277 so n = 4. F = 4, L = 3. To determine J and K,

	76 928 302 277
(L) L = 3 so L^3 = 27	- 27
	76 928 302 25
(K) $3L^2K$ = 27K ends in 5, so K =5, 27K= 135	- 1 35
	76 928 300 9
(J) $3L^2J + 3LK^2$ = 27J + 225	- 22 5
	76 928 278 4
27J ends with 4 so J = 2 and 27J = 54	-5 4
	76 928 273

We stop further calculations as we have got our required digits. Hence, the **CR of 76928302277 = 4253.**

2. By division method: The above method is for perfect squares. If one cannot determine whether the number is an exact cube or not we can use the division method. The method can be better explained by some examples.

a) $\sqrt[3]{226981}$ =? ; groups = 226 981; n = 2

	(a^3)	$(3a^2b)$		
108 |	226	$_{10}9$	$_{1}8$	1
$(3a^2)$		-	$-3ab^2$	$-(b^3)$
			-18	-1
		109	0	0
	216	108	0	0
	6	1 .	0	0
	(a)	(b)		

Hence **CR = 61**

For n = 2, the sequence of digits of the cube = a^3 | $3a^2b$ | $3ab^2$ | b^3. The first group 226 is taken as a^3 and the nearest perfect cube is 216 = 6^3. So, the first quotient Q_1 = a = 6. 216 is deducted from 226 to give 10 as the Remainder(R_1) which is carried over to the first digit of the second group to get a Dividend(D) of 109. There will be no deductions here. The divisor is calculated a $3a^2$ = 108. We can consider this 109 as $3a^2b$ which when divided by $3a^2$(the divisor) will give us 'b' the second quotient. So the second quotient Q_2 = 1 and R_2 = 1. The D will now be 18. We now deduct $3ab^2 = 3*6*1^2 = 18$ from D. The modified D after deduction will be 0 and Q_3 = 0 and R_3 = 0. The next D is 1 now. From this deduct $b^3 = 1^3$. The modified D is 0 again, hence Q_4 = 0 and R_4 = 0. We finally have **CR = 61.00 and 226981 is a perfect cube**. The decimal point is placed after the first 2 quotient digits to satisfy n = 2.

b) $\sqrt[3]{143}$ =? ; group = 143, n = 1.
The nearest perfect cube to 143 is 125, a cube of 5. So, Q1 = 5 and R1 = 18. The divisor = 3*52 = 75.

75 |	143	$_{18}0$	$_{30}0$	$_{90}0$	$_{97}0$
		-	$-(3ab^2)$	$-(6abc + b^3)$	$-(3ac^2 + 3b^2c)$
		-	- 60	-128	- 84
		180	240	772	886......
	125	150	150	675	
	5.	2	2	9.......	

In the division above, the formula for cubing a 3 digit number is utilised for deduction purposes. The first whole digit of the CR is 5 or 'a'. For the decimal part, we take a series of 0s. R_1 is carried to the first 0, so D = 180. Since there are no deductions to be made, divide by 75 to get Q_2 = 2 or 'b' and R_2 = 30. R_2 carried to the next 0, so D = 300. Deduct $3ab^2$ = 60 from D and the modified dividend(MD) = 240. Dividing the MD results in Q_3 = 2 or 'c' and R_3 =90. Here, we do not take Q_3 as 3 which will result in 3*75 = 225 that is closer to the MD. The reason being the remainder then would be much smaller and hence result in a smaller dividend. The next deduction would give a number greater than the dividend and the difference would be a negative number. Therefore, we take the lesser quotient 2.

Deducting $(6abc + b^3)$ = 128 from the next D = 900, the MD = 772. Dividing, we get Q_4 = 9 and R_4 = 97. We can continue this division for as many digits required after the decimal point. Here, we have **CR = 5.299 and the cube 143 is an imperfect cube**.

c) $\sqrt[3]{21.5}$ =? ; group = 21, n = 1; Q1 = 2; and R1 = 13.

The CR of a decimal number can be determined by the division method. The grouping is done from the left of the decimal point for the whole number and from the right of the decimal point for the decimal part.

12 |	21. |	$_{13}5$	$_{51}0$	$_{108}0$
		-	**$-3ab^2$**	**$-(6abc + b^3)$**
		-	-294	- 721
		135	216	359
	8	84	108	108
	2.	7	9	9...... **CR = 2.799...**

The division above is called the **'single-digit' division method** where each digit of the cube, except for the first group of 3 digits is divided individually. We can recap the division in the following manner:

For n = 2, the maximum digits in the cube(N) = 2*3 = 6. The first group will hold 3 digits and the remaining 3 digits will have 3 division steps. The sequence will be:

Division steps	Cube sequence	Deduction	Divisor	Quotient
-	a^3	-	-	a
1	$3a^2b$	-	$3a^2$	b.
2	$3ab^2$	$3ab^2$	$3a^2$	p
3	b^3	b^3	$3a^2$	q

Here, **CR = ab.**pq. The whole number part of the CR is ab and the decimal part is pq. If the value of pq = 00, the cube is a perfect cube or else it is an imperfect cube.

For n = 3, CR = abc, N = 3*3 = 9. Total division steps = 9 – 3 = 6

Division steps	Cube sequence	Deduction	Divisor	Quotient
-	a^3	-	-	a
1	$3a^2b$	-	$3a^2$	b
2	$3a^2c + 3ab^2$	$3ab^2$	$3a^2$	c
3	$b^3 + 6abc$	$b^3 + 6abc$	$3a^2$	p
4	$3ac^2 + 3b^2c$	$3a^2c + 3b^2c$	$3a^2$	q
5	$3bc^2$	$3bc^2$	$3a^2$	r
6	c^3	c^3	$3a^2$	s

Therefore, **CR = abc.**pqrs.

For n = 4, CR = abcd, N = 4*3 = 12, total division steps = 12 – 3 = 9.

Division steps	Cube sequence	Deduction	Divisor	Quotient
-	a^3	-	-	**a**
1	$3a^2b$	-	$3a^2$	**b**
2	$3a^2c + 3ab^2$	$3ab^2$	$3a^2$	**c**
3	$3a^2d + b^3 + 6abc$	$b^3 + 6abc$	$3a^2$	**d**
4	$6abd + 3ac^2 + 3b^2c$	$6abd + 3ac^2 + 3b^2c$	$3a^2$	p
5	$6acd + 3bc^2 + 3b^2d$	$6acd + 3bc^2 + 3b^2d$	$3a^2$	q
6	$6bcd + 3ad^2 + c^3$	$6bcd + 3ad^2 + c^3$	$3a^2$	r
7	$3bd^2 + 3c^2d$	$3bd^2 + 3c^2d$	$3a^2$	s
8	$3cd^2$	$3cd^2$	$3a^2$	t
9	d^3	d^3	$3a^2$	u

From the above table, **CR = abcd**.pqrstu.

To facilitate long division processes, we can approach the method using a **'two-digit' division method**. In this case, we carry out a preliminary calculation to find 'a' and 'b', after which both are clubbed together as 'a'. so 'n' will be reduced by 1 thus saving 3 division steps. For e.g. In $\sqrt[3]{12278428443}$; groups = 12 278 428 443, n = 4.

Using the two-digit method of division, the **preliminary calculation** will be

12 |	12	$_{4}2$	7	8
$(3a^2)$		42		
	8	36		
	2	**3**		
	(a)	(b).		

We will now take 23 as the new 'a', then n = 4 – 1 = 3.
The new divisor = $3*23^2 = 1587$

1587 |	12278	$_{111}4$	$_{1114}2$	$_{33}8$	$_{338}4$	$_{3}4$	$_{34}3$
$(3a^2)$			**$-3ab$**	**$-(b^3+6abc)$**	**$-(3ac^2+3b^2c)$**	**$-3bc^2$**	**$-c^3$**
		-	0	0	-3381	0	-343
		1114	11142	338	3	34	0
	12167	0	11109	0	0	0	0
	23	**0**	7.	0	0	0	0
	(a)	(b)	(c)				

Hence, **CR = 2307 and the cube is an exact cube**.

Chapter 13.

BEEJANK/ DIGIT SUM CHECK

The '**Digit Sum**' or '**Beejank**' or **Digital Root**' or '**Navashesha**' method is used to check on sums after operations to verify the answers. To use the said method one must understand the concept of a digit sum. As the name suggests, it is the addition of all digits of a number in use in the operation. Hence, the digit sum of a number, say, **346754 = 3 + 4 + 6 + 7 + 5 + 4 = 29 = 2 + 9 = 11 = 1 + 1 = 2.** The numbers are added over and over again till we obtain a single digit sum. Some important points to remember for the digit sum are :

1) The digit sum is always single digit number and is always positive.

2) A short cut method of addition is to ignore digits that are 9's or sums of 9 (*navashesha*), as they do not affect the outcome of the addition. For example, in the number given above i.e. 346754, 3 + 6 and 5 + 4 equalling 9 are ignored and the leftover digits 4 + 7 = 11 = 1 + 1 = 2.

3) The verification of the answer is done by using the same operation on the digit sums of the numbers in use for the said operation. For example, in the multiplication of two numbers say, 867 * 34, the solution is 29478. To verify the answer we first take the digit sums of 867, 34 and 29478 which are 3 ,7 and 3 respectively. On multiplying 3 * 7 we get 21 = 3 = same as the product. Hence the sum is correct.

   The sub-sutra used here is '**Gunitasamucchaya Samucchayagunitah**' (*the product of the sum is the sum of the products*). The same subsutra is used in addition as *the total of the digit sum is the digit sum of the total.*

4) The digit sum is not always a perfect checking device as it does not take into account human error in reporting. Thus, if an answer is 112 and one writes it as 121, in both cases, the digit sum is 4 but the answer is wrong.

Digit Sum check in :

1. **Addition**: While verifying the answer for an addition operation of two numbers, the digit sum of both the numbers have to be determined and these are added. The sum of these numbers, when converted to a digit sum, should equal the digit sum of the answer sum of the operation.

   Example 1: Add 4567 + 3245.

4567	Digit Sum = 4
+3245	Digit Sum = +5
7812	Digit Sum = 9

   Example 2: Add 657843 + 453432.

657843	Digit Sum = 6
+453432	Digit Sum = +3
1111275	Digit Sum = 9

   Practice Exercise: Carry out the digit sum check on all problems given in the Addition chapter and verify your answers.

2. **Subtraction**: To carry out an answer check of a subtraction operation, find the digit sums of the minuend, subtrahend and difference obtained. Subtracting the digit sum of the minuend and that of the subtrahend will result in the digit sum of the difference.

Example 1: Subtract 7765 – 4325.

	7765	Digit Sum = 7
-	4325	Digit Sum = -5
	3440	Digit Sum = 2

Example 2: Subtract 58943- 24638.

	58943	Digit Sum = 2
-	24638	Digit Sum = -5
	34305	Digit Sum = 6 (2 -5 = -3=> 9 + (-3) = 6)

- An important point to remember while carrying out an operation on digit sums is that when we get a negative answer, we can covert the same to a positive number by adding a 9 to the negative number.

Practice Exercises: Verify answers of all sums given in the Subtraction Chapter using the digit sum method.

3. **Multiplication**: Multiplying the digit sum of the multiplicand and that of the multiplier should be the digit sum of the product.

Example: Multiply 345 * 34.

345	Digit Sum = 3
x34	Digit Sum = x7
11730	Digit Sum = 3 (3*7 = 21 = 3)

Practice Set: Verify the solutions of all problems given in the Multiplication Chapter.

4. **Division**: The common formula for checking the answer of a division operation is as follows:

Dividend = Quotient * Divisor + Remainder.
This is the same formula that will be used taking the digit sums of the dividend, divisor, quotient and remainder.

Example: Divide 849 ÷ 7
849 ÷ 7 = Quotient is 121 remainder is 2.
Verifying, 3(digit sum of 849) = 4(digit sum of 121)*7 + 2
Therefore, 3 = 1 + 2 = 3. Verified.

Practice: Verify all solutions from Division chapter.

Chapter 14.

BHAJAKATVA / DIVISIBILITY

Divisibility test is carried out to see if a number is divisible by a particular divisor. The divisibility check for small divisors are:

1. A number is divisible by 2 if it is an even number i.e. if the last digit of the number is 0, 2, 4, 6, or 8.

2. A number is divisible by 3 if the Single Digit Sum (SDS) is equal to 3, 6 or 9 (0 as 9 is considered as 0). For e.g. Is 2091 divisible by 3 ? The SDS of 2091 = 2 + 0 + 9 +1 = 3. Therefore, 2091 is divisible by 3.

3. A number is divisible by 4 if the last 2 digits of the number is divisible by 4. For e.g. The number 1964 has 64 as the last 2 digits and 16*4 =64. So, 1964 is divisible by 4.

4. A number is divisible by 5 if the number ends in '0' or '5'.

5. A number is divisible by 6 if the number is even and its SDS is 3, 6 or 9(0). For e.g. the number 3258 is an even number and its SDS = 9 or 0. Hence it is divisible by 6.

6. When the last digit of a number is doubled and subtracted from the rest of the number and the difference is 0 or a multiple of 7, the number is divisible by 7. For e.g. in the number 238, twice the last digit is 8*2 = 16. When 16 is subtracted from the rest of the number i.e. 23 the difference is 23 – 16 = 7. Therefore, 238 is divisible by 7.

7. A number is divisible by 8 if the last 3 digits of the number is divisible by 8. For e.g. in 5328, the last 3 digits 328 = 8 * 41. Hence, 5328 is divisible by 8.

8. If the SDS of a number is 0 or 9, then the number is divisible by 9.

9. If the difference between the sum of the odd digits and sum of even digits of a number is 0 or a multiple of 11, then it is divisible by 11.

Checking for divisibility by the Osculation Method:

The divisibility test for bigger divisors, up to 2 digits, involves the use of the sub-sutra **Veshtanam** translating as ***by osculation***. The method employed is to find the positive(P) and negative(Q) osculators or ***veshtanas*** of the divisor.

The positive veshtana or osculator is also called the **Ekadhika** (from the sutra Ekadhikena Purvena or *by one more than the previous*). The divisor has to be a number with 9 as its last digit. For example the divisor 19 has 9 as the last digit, so the ekadhika is considered by dropping 9 and adding 1 to the digit before 9. Hence the ekadhika (P) of 19 is 2.

If the divisor doesn't end in 9, then to find P, we multiply the divisor by the smallest number to get a product having 9 as the unit digit. We then add 1 and divide by 10, to get the value of P. Algebraically, if 'n' is the divisor, 'k' is the smallest multiplier, then **P = (nk +1)/10** is the positive osculator or ekadhika.

The negative osculator (Q),also called the **Viparita**, is calculated when the units place digit of the divisor is 1. In this case, the 1 is dropped and the number before it is considered to be the negative osculator. For e.g. if 41 is the divisor, then Q = 4.

If however, the divisor doesn't end in 1 then to find Q, we multiply the divisor 'n' by the smallest number 'k' to get a product having 1 as the unit digit. We then subtract 1 from the product and divide by 10 to get Q. Therefore, **Q = (nk – 1)/10** is the negative osculator. An important point to remember is that **n = P + Q.**

To check for divisibility, we need to select the appropriate osculator and keep multiplying the unit digit of the dividend and adding or subtracting from the rest of the number. We continue in this manner till all digits of the dividend are covered. If the final answer is 0 or a multiple of the divisor, the dividend is divisible by the divisor. In the case of Q, the dividend is grouped in such a way that every alternate digit from the right is considered as a vinculum or bar number.

Example: Is 123459 divisible by 7?

The first step is to find the osculators. P =7(7) +1/10 = 5 and Q = 2 and 5 + 2 = 7. Since both osculators are small numbers, we can use either to check for divisibility in the following way:

Using P, 12345~~9~~ x 5
= +45
= 12390 x 5
+ 0
= 123~~9~~ x 5
= +45
= 16~~8~~ x 5
= +40
= 56 (multiple of 7 as 7*8 = 56)

Therefore, 123459 is divisible by 7.

Using Q, $\bar{1}2\bar{3}4\bar{5}9$ × 2
(2*9 -5 = 13) x 2
(2*3 -1 + 4 = 9) x 2
(2*9 -0 +(-3) = 15) x 2
(2*5 -1 + 2 = 11) x 2
(2*1 -1 +(-1) = 0)

Since the end result is 0, the number is divisible by 7.

Depending on the complexity of P or Q, one can decide to utilise either one.

Practice exercises: a) Is 6603 divisible by 31? b) Is 11234 divisible by 41? c) Is 742165 divisible by 47? d) Is 14061 divisible by 43? e) Is 21953 divisible by 53? f) Is 63094821 divisible by 79?

Using complex osculators:

So far we have dealt with fairly small and simple divisors and therefore smaller osculators. If the divisor is of 3 or more digits, the divisibility will be done by grouping the dividend into groups of 2 or more digits taken together to ease the process.

For e.g for the divisor 499, $P_2 = (499 + 1)/100 = 5$. The positive osculator will be 5 and the dividend will be grouped in 2 digits. For dividend 61377, the groups will be 6, 13 and 77 respectively and by osculation with $P_2 = 5$,

6 13 77 x 5

= +3 85

= 9 98 x 5

= +490

= 499 therefore, the number is by divisible by 499.

Some observations:

1. The subscript to P or Q (in this case P2) will indicate the group size of the dividend (in case above being 2).

2. Also, the size of the base divisor for P and Q (100 in this case) also indicates the subscript number of P and Q. For e.g. for the

divisor 5001, Q_3 =5, for 799999, P_5 = 8 and will have groups of 3 digits and 5 digits respectively in their dividends.

Some examples:

1) Is 1928264569 divisible by 5999?
   Here P3 = 6,

$$
\begin{array}{lrrrl}
 & 1 & 928 & 264 & 569 \text{ x6} \\
= & & & +3 & \underline{414} \\
= & 1 & 931 & 678 & \text{x } 6 \\
= & +4 & \underline{068} & & \\
= & 5 & 999 & &
\end{array}
$$

the result is 5999, so the number is divisible by 5999.

2) Is 21886068313597 divisible by 7001?
   In this case Q3 = 7,

$$21 \quad \overline{886} \quad 068 \quad \overline{313} \quad 597 \times 7$$

= (4179 – 313 = 3866) x 7

= (6062 -3 + 68 = 6127) x 7

= (889 -6 – 886 = -3) x 7

= (-21 + 21 = 0)

Therefore, the number is divisible by 7001.

Practice exercises: a) Is 106656874269 divisible by 499? b) Is 126143622932 divisible by 401? c) Is 69492392 divisible by 199? d) Is 2130110211434112 divisible by 999? e) Is 5246766400162014552 divisible by 1001?

Chapter 15.

MULTIPLICATION TABLES CREATION

While studying modern mathematics, a student is burdened with memorizing the multiplication tables of up to 30. Vedic Mathematics, however, expects the student to know the table up to 5 only. The rest of the tables can be calculated in a matter of minutes using the addition and subtraction ('Vinculum') methods. Let us take a look at how this is done with single digits greater than 5, two digit numbers and three digit numbers.

Multiplication table of a 1 digit number:

The first step is to observe if the number is less than or equal to 5. If not, then convert the number whose multiplication table we are creating, into a Vinculum number. Let us take an example for creating the table of 6 which is a single digit and greater than 5.

To convert 6 into a vinculum number, 6 = 10 – 4 = +1 in the tens place and -4 in the units place. The multiplication table is created by repeatedly adding + 1 to the tens place number and subtracting 4 from the units place number.

During the subsequent addition and subtraction, we will encounter a vinculum number. This can be easily converted to a normal number with the help of the 'Ekanyunena Purvena' (by one less than the previous) and Nikhilam (all from nine and last from 10) Sutras that state that the tens place digit is to be reduced by 1 and the negative units digit's complement number from 10 is taken. For example, 6 * 3 = (1 + 1) | (2 – 4) = 2 | -2 = vinculum number.
2 | -2 = (2 – 1) | (10 -2) = 18. Hence, 6 * 3 = 18.

Let us depict this as a table:

6 * table	Vinculum number	+1 -4
6 * 1 =		0 6
6 * 2 =		1 2
6 * 3 =	2 | -2	1 8
6 * 4 =		2 4
6 * 5 =		3 0
6 * 6 =	4 | -4	3 6
6 * 7 =		4 2
6 * 8 =	5 | -2	4 8
6 * 9 =		5 4
6 * 10 =		6 0

Multiplication table of a 2 digit number:

Case 1: If the units digit is less than or equal to 5, the addition method is used. For example, in the number 64, the units digit is < 5. Therefore the number can be written as +6 +4 and these are to be added repeatedly to the tens place number and units place number to create the table. During the process there will be carrying numbers in the units place and have to be balanced accordingly. Let us create a multiplication table of 64.

64 * table	Carrying numbers	+6 +4
64 * 1		6 4
64 * 2		12 8
64 * 3	18 | 12	19 2
64 * 4		25 6
64 * 5	31 | 10	32 0
64 * 6		38 4
64 * 7		44 8
64 * 8	50 | 12	51 2
64 * 9		57 6
64 * 10	63 | 10	64 0

Case 2: If the units digit is > 5, the vinculum method is used. As before, the number is converted to a vinculum number. Taking an example of 88 where the units digit is greater than 5. Then 88 = 90 – 2 = +9 -2.

88 * table	**Vinculum number**	**+9 -2**
88 * 1		8 8
88 * 2		17 6
88 * 3		26 4
88 * 4		35 2
88 * 5		44 0
88 * 6	53 | -2	52 8
88 * 7		61 6
88 * 8		70 4
88 * 9		79 2
88 * 10		88 0

Practice Exercises: a) Create multiplication tables from 1 to 100. And b) Try tables with 3 digit numbers.

Chapter 16.

CALENDAR CALCULATIONS

A calendar is a system devised to organise time into aptly named fixed periods and for marking the beginning and end of a period as a physical record. It comprises a list that shows the 'days', 'weeks' and 'months' of a particular 'year'. While referring to a calendar, one mentions a 'date' which represents a single specific day in such a system.

Periods of a Calendar:

1) **Date:** 26th April, 2015, as an example is how a date appears. On examination, one can understand that it is the 26th 'day' of the 'month' of April in the 'year' 2015. Breaking down the year further, the first 2 digits represent the century year, in this case 2000 and the last 2 digits the 15th year of this century.
2) **Year:** A year is the time taken by Earth to complete a full orbit of the Sun. It has been calculated to be 365 days and 6 hours. For calculation purposes, a **Normal Year** (henceforth represented as NY) consists of 365 days. The extra 6 hours, taken collectively over a period of 4 years completes a 24 hour day. As a result, there is an extra day in the calendar every 4 years. This year, with 366 days, is called a **Leap Year** (LY).
3) **Day:** A day is the smallest unit of the calendar consisting of 24 hours which is the time taken for the Moon to complete an orbit around the Earth.
4) **Week:** A period of 7 days is called a week. Hence in a NY there are 365/7 or 52 weeks and an extra day. In a LY, there are 366/7 or 52 weeks and 2 extra days.

   The names of the days of the week can be presented as follows:

Day Code	Name of Day
0	Sunday
1	Monday
2	Tuesday
3	Wednesday
4	Thursday
5	Friday
6	Saturday

5) **Month:** A year is organised into 12 months. Each month alternately consists of 31 and 30 days. The exception is the second month, February which has 28 days in a NY and 29days in a LY. The other exception is the 7th and 8th month both of which have 31 days. Each month comprises of 4 weeks and some extra days. The table below explains this in a better way.

Month name	No. of days	Extra days
January	31	3
February	28/29	0/1
March	31	3
April	30	2
May	31	3
June	30	2
July	31	3
August	31	3
September	30	2
October	31	3
November	30	2
December	31	3
Total:	**365/366**	**29/30**

The extra days add up to 4 weeks and 1 or 2 extra days denoting the type of year.

Important points in Calculation:

1) While considering the year for calculation purposes we have understood the normal year and the leap year. There is one more type of year we have to take note of. This is the **Century Year** (CY). A century year is a year whose last 2 digits are zeros depicting the century. So the years 100, 200,300,.....1600, 1700, 1800, 1900 etc. are all CYs. Th CYs that are divisible by 400 are called Leap Century Years (LCY). Therefore, 400, 800, 1200, 1600, 2000 etc. are LCYs.

   There are 24 leap years in a CY and 25 leap years in a LCY. So 29th February appears 24 times in 100 years and 97 times (24*3 + 25) in 400 years. Also, the 29th of all months appears 1124 (24 LY*12 (29th s in a LY) + 76 NY *11(29th s in a NY)) times in 100 years and 4497 times in 400 years.

   The number of extra days in a LY is 2 and in a NY is 1. Then, in a 100 years, the number of extra days can be calculated as 24 * 2 = 48 extra day in all leap years and 76*1 = 76 extra days in the normal years, totalling to 124. Since the number of extra days cannot exceed 7(it becomes a wee, otherwise), we divide 124 by 7. This gives us a quotient of 17 and a remainder of 5. This indicates 17 weeks and 5 extra days.

   Hence, number of extra days in 100 years = **5**
   Number of extra days in 200 years = 5*2 = 10/7= **3**
   Number of extra days in 300 years = 5*3 = 15/7= **1**
   Number of extra days in 400 years = 5*4 =20 +1(LCY)/7 = **0**

   Continuing forward, the sequence of 5, 3, 1, 0 will repeat after every LCY. The year 500, when divided by

400 leaves a remainder of 100 hence it will have 5 extra days and so on. All LCYs will have 0 extra days. This also reveals the fact that the calendar repeats itself every 400 years. For example, if 30th January, 2021, is a Saturday, then 30th January, 2421 and 30th January, 1621 will be a Saturday as well.

The number of extra days in a particular CY, will also reveal the last day of the century. For example the last day of 17th century, is 31st December,1700. The number of extra days in 1700 = 1600 + 100 = 0 + 5 =5. Referring to the day of the week table, 5 stands for Friday. So, the last day of 1700 falls on a Friday.

A year whose last 2 digits are NOT '0's and also NOT divisible by 4 is considered a normal or ordinary year consisting of 365 days. The first day of the NY is also the last day of the year. Hence, if 1st January, 2005 is a Monday, then 31st December, 2005 is also a Monday.

An important point to remember from above is that the century year will end only on 0, 1, 3 & 5 i.e. Sunday, Monday, Wednesday and Friday and NOT on 2,4,6 viz. Tuesday, Thursday and Saturday. The first day of the first year of the century can only begin with 1, 2, 4 and 6 and not with 0,3,5. Another observation from this is that the first and last day of a century can fall on a Monday (1).

One common mistake that a student makes in considering the first day of a century say 1700 will state that the first day is 1st January, 1700 which is incorrect as 1700 is the last year of the century. The correct day is 1st January, 1601.

2) For month calculations, points to remember are

   a) The month that has 29 days will have the same day as the first and last day. For e.g. in February of a leap year, if the first day of the month is Sunday, then the last day will be Sunday as well. The explanation is that 29/7 will have 1 extra day and 4 weeks. If the first day of the first week is Sunday, then the last day of the last week will be Saturday and the last extra day will be Sunday again. If it is a normal year the last day of February in this case will be Saturday as there are no extra days.

   b) If the month has 30 days, then the last of the month will be the next day after the day of the first day of the month. For e.g. if the first day of April of a particular year is a Sunday, then the penultimate day will be Sunday again and the last day will be Monday as there are 2 extra days in April.(refer to the month table)

   c) If the month has 31 days then the last day will be 2 days after the first day.

3) Repetition of a calendar: example: If 5th March, 2006 is a Monday, then which year's 5th March will fall on a Monday?

To solve the problem posed above we have to use the following calculations:

Step 1: Divide the year (last 2 digits) by 4. We get the remainders{ 0,1,2,3}

Step 2: If remainder = 0, add 28
remainder = 1, add 6
remainder = 2, add 11
remainder = 3, add 11 to the given year.

In the case above, 06/4 gives a remainder of 2 so 2006 + 11 = 2017. Therefore 5th March, 2017 will fall on a Monday.

The exception in the above is if the date fall in January and February. Then a partial repetition occurs earlier than 2017. If the date was 5th February, 2006 instead, we calculate the extra days in the following years till we get 7 extra days. The solution will be the following year. For e.g. 2006 = 1 day, 2007 = 1 day, 2008 =2 days, 2009 = 1 day, 2010 = 1 day, 2011= 1 day. Adding the extra days we get 7. So there will be a partial repetition of the calendar as 5th February, 2012 will fall on a Monday.

Calculating and predicting the day of a particular date:

Problem: What day is 15th March, 1925?

Solution:

1) Calculate the extra days in the previous completed year. In this case, 1924 = 1900 + 24 + 6 (leap years) = 1600 + 300 + 30 = 0 + 1 + 30 = 31
2) Count the extra days in the present year so far = extra days in January, February and 15 days of March = 3 + 0 + 15 =18
3) Add up all the odd days = 31 + 18 = 49
4) Divide the sum by 7 = 49/7 = remainder is 0. Hence, it is a **Sunday.**

Calculating using a formula:

All the information given above was for acquainting the student with the logic behind the calendar. There is, however, another method to solve the above problem using a formula. For that there are certain codes that the student needs to commit to memory. The codes are as follows:

1) **Century year codes:**

Century code	**6**	**4**	**2**	**0**
Year	0	100	200	300
	400	500	600	700
	800	900	1000	1100
	1200	1300	1400	1500
	1600	1700	1800	1900
	2000	2100	2200	2300

2) **Month Codes:**

Month	**Code**	**Month**	**Code**	**Month**	**Code**
January	0	May	1	September	5
February	3	June	4	October	0
March	3	July	6	November	3
April	6	August	2	December	5

3) **Year code**: There are no year codes. But in calculating, we need the number of leap years in the year so far that can be obtained by dividing the last 2 digits of the year year by 4. Another point to remember is that if the date falls in January/ February of a leap year we have to add -1 to the sum.

4) **The formula**: Day (D) + Month Code (MC) + Century Code (CC) + Number of Leap years + last 2 digits of the year = sum (-1 if date is in Jan/Feb of a leap year) /7= Remainder { day}

Example 1: What day was it on 15th August, 1947?

According to formula, D = 15, MC = 2, CC = 0, Number of Leap years = 47/4 = 11(ignore the remainder) and last digits of year = 47. Adding the same =15 + 2 + 0 + 11 + 47 = 75/7 = remainder { 5 = Friday}. Therefore, 15th August, 1947, fell on a Friday.

Example 2: What day was 12th November, 1964?

12 (D) + 3 (MC) + 0 (CC) + 16 (LY) + 64 (Y) = 95 / 7 = Remainder =4 = Thursday.

CHAPTER 17

CLOCK CALCULATIONS

A clock is a physical system designed to observe the time of a day. The face of a clock is circular and divided into 12 equal time units denoting the hour from 1 to 12 of the daylight hours and again from 1 to 12 of the evening and nightfall hours. Since a full circle comprises of 360 degrees, each hour unit is made up of 360 / 12 = 30 degrees each. At the centre of the clock, are 3 arrows of different sizes. The largest arrow, also the fastest, is called the 'Seconds Hand' and indicates the number of seconds. The second, smaller arrow called the ' Minute Hand' moves slower than the seconds hand and shows the exact minute of the hour. The third, as well as the slowest arrow called the ' Hour Hand' indicates the hour of the day.

A 24 hour day is divided into 12 daylight hours and indicated as A.M. () and 12 night time hours indicated as P.M.(). In some cases the time is stated as '….00' hours. For e.g. 5 P.M. is called 1700 hours. The last two digits are indicative of the minutes in that hour. Say, 5: 45 P.M. is also 1745 hours. Additionally, 5 A.M is 0500 hours.

Some concepts:

a) In 1 minute, the seconds hand (SH) will rotate a full 360° and in 1 hour the minute hand (MH) moves 360° as well.

b) The 12 equal time units or hours make up 360°. So 1 hour = 360° /12 =30°. This 30° is dived equally into 5 parts, each equalling 6°. So each hand of the clock moves at the rate of 6°. The SH moves over the 12*5 = 60 parts in 1 minute and the minute hand moves over 60 parts in 1 hour. Hence 1 minute(or 1') = 60 seconds (or 60") and 1 hour = 60 minutes or 3600 seconds.

c) In 1 hour the MH moves 360°. In the meantime, the HH moves as well. The HH completes 360° in 12 hours.
So, 12 * 60' = 720' =360° => 1'= 360 / 720 = ½ °.
Therefore, for every move the MH makes in a minute, the HH moves ½ °.

Calculations:

Calculations are normally carried out to find the positions of the MH and HH, and the angle (θ) between them at any given time of a perfectly working clock and also to calculate the loss or gain in display of time of a faulty clock.

1) **To find the angle between the MH and HH at any given time**: There is a formula to do such calculation as given below:

θ = [30H -11/2M] where θ is the angle between the MH and HH, H indicates the hour and M, the minutes. A few things to remember are if the solution is negative or positive, the answer remains the same and if the solution is greater than 180°, then the true answer can be obtained by subtracting 180° from the solution, as the greater angle is indicative of the reflex angle formed outside.

Example 1 : Find the angle between MH and HH at 5:40.

Solution: θ = [30*5 – 11*40/2]° = [150 – 220]° =[-70]° = **70°**

Explanation: At 5, the HH will be at 5 at 5*30 =150° and the MH will be on 12.
At 5:40, the MH will move to 8 i.e. 8*30°= 240°.
The HH moves 1/2° every minute then it moves ½ * 40 = 20°. Therefore, the HH will be 150 + 20 = 170°from 12 and

the MH at 240°from 12. Hence, the angle between the MH and HH at 5:40 = 240 -170 = 70°.

Example 2: Find angle between the MH and HH at 1:20

Solution: θ =[30*1 – 11*20/2] = [30 – 110] = **80°**

2) **To find the time in minutes when the MH and HH are together i.e. θ = 0°**. The most important concept to understand here, is that, the clock is divided into 60 minute spaces, 5 minute spaces for each hour. In 1 hour the MH moves 60 minute spaces whereas the HH moves only 5 minute spaces. Therefore, the MH gains 55 minute spaces in 60 minutes. In this case, θ = 0, H will be the hour in which the two hands are together and M will be the minutes past the hour H when they are together.

   Example : When will the MH and HH overlap between 3 and 4 '0' clock?

   Solution: [30* 3 – 11*M/2] = 0; or [90 – 11M/2] = 0; or M = 90*2/ 11 = 180/11; or M = **16 and 4/11 minutes past 3.**

   Explanation: At 3, the HH will be at 3 or 15 minute spaces from 12 and the MH will have to move past at least 15 minute spaces to reach the HH and then some more spaces to overlap the HH. If 55 minute spaces = 60 minutes, then 15 minute spaces = 60*15/55 = 180/11 = 16 and 4/11 minutes. Therefore, at 16 and 4/11 minutes past 3 will be the time when the hands are together.

3) **To find the time when the HH and MH are opposite to each other and θ = 180°**

Example : At what time between 7 and 8'o'clock will the MH and HH be opposite to each other?

Solution: [30*7 – 11M/2] =180; or M = (210 – 180)*2/11 = 60/11 = **5 and5/11 minutes past 7**.

Explanation: At 7 or a little after it, the HH will be at 7 and for the MH to be in the opposite direction, it has to be between 1 and 2. So the MH moves at least 5 minute spaces and more. So the time will be (60*5)/55 = 60/11 = 5 and 5/11 minutes. Therefore, the two hands will lie opposite to each other at 5 5/11 mins past 7.

4) **To find the time when MH and HH are perpendicular to each other and θ = 90°**.

There will be two possible answers to this calculation as the MH could be 90° behind the HH or ahead of it. If the MH is behind, θ = +90°and, if ahead, θ = -90°. To solve, draw the HH between the beginning and end of the hour and draw a perpendicular line from the HH stretching on both sides of the HH. This will give the positions of the MH before and after the HH. Calculate using the formula with separate values of θ.

Example : At what time between 7 & 8 'o' clock will the MH be perpendicular to the HH ?

Solution : [30*7 – 11M/2] = 90 and [30*7 – 11M/2] = -90 => M= {(210 – 90)*2}/11 and M = { (210 + 90)*2}/11. => M= 240/11 or 21 and 9/11 mins and M = 600/11 or 54 and 6/11 mins. Therefore, the MH will be perpendicular to the HH at 21 and 9/11 minutes past 7 and 54 and 6/11 mins past 7.

5) **To find the time at a particular hour when the MH and HH are a specified number of minutes apart**. The number of minutes apart may be calculated by multiplying it with 6°, as 1 minute equals 6°. This will give the value of θ. The hour is given so we can calculate the M. Here too, there will be two solutions as the minutes apart could be before or after the HH.

Example: At what time between 3 and 4 will the MH and HH be 4 minutes apart?

Solution: θ = 4*6 = 24°. It could be +ve and -ve.
[30*3 – 11M/2] = 24 and [30*3 – 11M/2] = -24
Or M = {(90 – 24)*2}/11 and M = {(90 + 24)*2}/11
Or M = 132/11 = 12 and M = 228/11 = 20 and 8/11.

Therefore, between 3 and 4 'o'clock, the MH and HH will be 4 minutes apart at **12 past 3** and once again, at **20 and 8/11 past 3**.

6) **To find the incorrect time displayed with a faulty clock.** The clock could be running slow/fast or in other words, losing/ gaining minutes or seconds per hour thus displaying an erratic time. The method carried out is to multiply the **gain/loss** per hour by the difference of the required correct time and the time when the clock was set correctly and subtracting/ adding the result to the required time.

Example 1: If a clock is set right at 5 a.m. and the clock gains 5 minutes every hour, what time will be displayed at 10 a.m. ?

Solution: The time lapsed from 5 a.m. to 10 a.m. will be 10 – 5 = 5 hours.

The clock gains 5 minutes in 1 hour.

Therefore, minutes gained in 5 hours = 5*5 = 25 minutes

So, the time displayed will be **10:25 a.m.** instead of 10:00 a.m.

Example 2: A clock is set right at 7:00 a.m.. The clock loses 5 seconds every hour. What time will be displayed at 2 p.m. ?

Solution: The time lapsed from 7 a.m. and 2 p.m. = 7 hours
The clock loses 5 seconds every hour.
So, time lost in 7 hours = 7*5 = 35 seconds.
Incorrect time displayed at 2p.m. = **1:59:25** p.m.

Sutra	***Translation***
1. Ekadhikena Purvena	*By one more than the one before*
2. Nikhilam Navadashatah Charmam	*All from 9 last from 10*
3. Urdhva Tiryagbhyaam	*Vertically and crosswise*
4. Paravartya Yojayet	*Transpose and apply*
5. Shunyam Saamyasamuchhayeh	*If Samuchhaya is same it is 0*
6. Aanurupyeh Shunyam Anyat	*If one is in ratio other is 0*
7. Sankalana Vyavakalanaabhyaam	*By addition and by subtraction*
8. Puranaapuranabhyaam	*By completion and non-completion*
9. Chalana Kalanaabhyaam	*Differential Calculus*
10. Yaavadunam	*By the deficiency*
11. Vyashtsamashtih	*Specific and general*
12. Sheshanyankena Charamena	*The remainders by the last digit*

13. Sopaantyadayamantyam *The ultimate and twice the penultimate*

14. Ekanyunena Purvena *By one less than the one before*

15.Gunitahsamuchhayah *The product of the sum*

16. Gunakasamuchhayah *All the multipliers*

Upasutra ***Translation***

1. ***Anurupyena*** *Proportionately*

2. Shishyate Sheshsangyah *The remainder remains constant*

3. Aadhyamaadhyennaantyamantyen *The first by the first, last by the last*

4. Kevalaih Saptakam Gunyat *For 7 the multiplicand is 143*

5. Veshtanam *Osculation*

6. Yaavadunam Taavadunam *Lessen by the Deficiency*

7. Yaavadunam Taavadunikritya Vargancha Yojayet *Lessen by deficiency and set up square of deficiency.*

8. Antyayordashakepi *Last totalling 10*

9. Antyayoreva *Only the last terms*

10. Samuchhayagunitah *The sum of the products*

11. Lopanasthapanaabhyam *By alternate elimination and retention*

12. Vilokanam *By mere observation*

13. Gunitasamuchhayah Samuchhayagunitah *The product of the sum is the sum of the product.*

REFERENCES:

1. Kenneth R. Williams ,Vedic Mathematics- Teacher's Manual (Intermediate level) published by Motilal Banarasidass, First Indian Edition: Delhi 2005. ISBN 978-81-208-2787-5.

2. Kenneth R. Williams ,Vedic Mathematics- Teacher's Manual (Advanced level) published by Motilal Banarasidass, First Indian Edition: Delhi 2005. ISBN 978-81-208-2776-9.

3. Sri Bharati Krsna Tirthaji Maharaja, Vedic Mathematics, published by Motilal Banarasidass, 19th Reprint, 2019. ISBN 978-81-208-0164-6.

About the Author:

Priti Gorsia Chawla was born in Calcutta (now Kolkata) in 1963. Growing up, she studied Core Mathematics till Higher Secondary Level. Over the next 15 years, she taught mathematics, informally, across all school boards while running her Interior design business.

She came across Vedic Mathematics when she attended a few workshops with the legendary Shakuntala Devi, while in her school years, and has been, ever since, exploring the subject.

She moved to Mumbai, in 1992, after her marriage. As a housewife, she continued to teach maths and also developed a keen interest in cooking, naturopathy and cosmetology. Over the years, she has written four cookbooks that will soon be released as well.

She is also keenly interested in music, crosswords, sudoku, sports like tennis, squash and swimming.

She is a qualified Vedic Maths trainer and this is her first book on the subject.

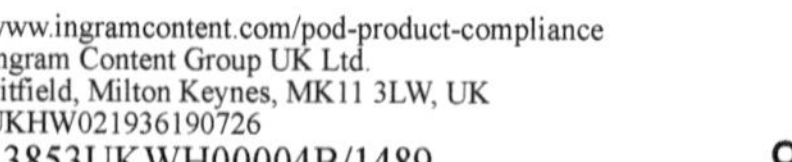

www.ingramcontent.com/pod-product-compliance
Ingram Content Group UK Ltd.
Pitfield, Milton Keynes, MK11 3LW, UK
UKHW021936190726
13853UKWH00004B/1489

9 789356 111868